MW01289289

Dari Grammar
and
Phrase Book

DARI GRAMMAR AND PHRASE BOOK

Ehsan M. Entezar

Copyright © 2010 by Ehsan M. Entezar.

Library of Congress Control Number:		2010906550
ISBN:	Hardcover	978-1-4500-9931-8
	Softcover	978-1-4500-9930-1
	Ebook	978-1-4500-9932-5

All rights reserved. No part of this book may be reproduced or transmitted
in any form or by any means, electronic or mechanical, including photocopying,
recording, or by any information storage and retrieval system,
without permission in writing from the copyright owner.

This book was printed in the United States of America.

To order additional copies of this book, contact:
Xlibris Corporation
1-888-795-4274
www.Xlibris.com
Orders@Xlibris.com
76588

Contents

Pronunciation Guide

Symbol	Dari	English
/a/	/as/ "from"	ask
/aa/	/naan/ "bread"	far
/e/	/dest/ "hand"	get
/i/	/sir/ "garlic"	feet
/o/	/omr/ "age"	put
/u/	/zud/ "fast"	shoot
/ey/	/deyr/ "late"	day
/ow/	/zowr/ "force/power"	low
/aay/	/aayna/ "mirror"	I
/b/	/bad/ "bad"	best
/p/	/paak/ "clean"	pest
/t/	/tu/ "you"	test
/d/	/ dest/	den
/k/	/kaard/ "knife"	kin
/g/	/gaaz/ "swing"	get
/q/	/qaalin/ "rug"	None
/s/	/seyb/ "apple"	sent
/z/	/zan/ "wife/ woman"	was
/sh/	/shaar/ "city/town"	she
/zh/	/gazhdom/ "scorpion"	measure
/f/	/faarsi/ "Farsi"	Farsi

/kh/	/**kho**sh/ "happy"	none
/gh/	/af**gh**aan/ "Afghan"	none
/ch/	/**ch**aar "four"	**ch**est
/j/	/**j**aan/ "dear/body"	**j**ust
/m/	/**m**a/ "I"	**m**e
/n/	/**n**aam/ "name"	**n**ame
/l/	/ka**l**aan/ "big/large"	**l**earn
/r/	/**r**aa/ "path/way/road"	**r**ent
/w/	/**w**akht/ "time"	**w**ent
/y/	/**y**ak/ "one"	**y**es

PREFACE

Since 9/11 and the overthrow of the Taliban, more and more Westerners and people from Asia and other countries going to Afghanistan feel the need to learn Dari. The materials commercially available are mostly in the form of phrase books without any significant information the grammar of Dari. Additionally, the limited Dari grammar books available are mostly of the written instead of the spoken form of the language. As it will be made clear, spoken and written Dari are two different systems. Furthermore, these grammars are primarily prescriptive rather than descriptive in that instead of describing language as *it is (descriptive)*, they describe it as *it should be (prescriptive)*. This book is the first attempt to provide a descriptive grammar of spoken Dari.

My interest in language and language teaching is both theoretical and practical, going back to the 1960s. My doctorate is in applied linguistics and I have taught Dari grammar at Kabul University and in the Peace Corps. Additionally, I have written many articles on linguistics and language teaching. Between 1964 and 1969, I wrote several language textbooks for the United States Peace Corps: *Farsi (Afghan Persian)* (1964), The School for International Training, Putney, Vermont, USA; *Intermediate Dari* (1965), U.S. Peace Corps, Kabul and *Dari* (1969), The University of Texas at Austin.

Farsi (Afghan Persian) was the first attempt ever to teach spoken/ conversational Dari systematically to native speakers of English. It was based on the audio-lingual method, common in the 1960s. This approach to language teaching emphasized on listening and speaking rather than reading and writing skills, providing very little information on grammar in the process. The goal was to help Peace Corps volunteers communicate with ordinary Afghans. Therefore, the materials were presented in phonemic transcription and avoided any expressions (words, phrases, and sentences) of the written form of Dari. In short, *Farsi (Afghan Persian)* and subsequent manuals I wrote were to teach spoken Dari to Americans going to Afghanistan as Peace Corps volunteers.

Modern language teaching approaches are learner-centered, emphasizing language functions and an understanding of the target language structure (grammar). This book is a systematic attempt to provide an outline of spoken Dari grammar to assist individuals in learning to speak the language. Using this grammar as a reference, Americans and other Westerners can learn how to speak Dari with the help of informants (native Dari speakers), tutors, or on their own.

There are two parts to *Dari Grammar and Phrase book*. Part 1, grammar, deals with Dari sounds, verbs, nouns, adjectives, adverbs, prepositions, and clauses along with their formations, types, and functions. Part 2 phrase book consists of language functions and topics. More specifically, this part briefly discusses language functions: how to ask/give information, agree/disagree, persuade/dissuade, give commands and make suggestions, and so on. The topics include shopping and clothing, fruits and vegetables, travel and transportation, security, family and relations, education, health, religion and worship, and weather and climate. The book ends with three appendixes. Appendix A is about days of the week and months of the year; Appendix B covers ordinal and cardinal numbers, and Appendix C discusses Afghan names.

Dari Grammar and Phrase book would not have been completed without the support and encouragement of some individuals. First and foremost, I am indebted to Dr. Karl Krahnke, Professor of Linguistics, Colorado State University, an ex-Peace Corps volunteer in Afghanistan, for taking his valuable time to read the manuscript and make invaluable comments and criticisms. Professor Krahnke taught English to Afghan students and he is fluent in Dari. Additionally, I am also indebted to Doctors John Bing and Robert Pearson, also returned Peace Corps volunteers from Afghanistan, for their constant support and encouragement, and for reading the manuscript. Finally, I am grateful to my wife and children for their wholehearted support. While Professor Krahnke contributed comments and suggestions, I take the responsibility for any flaws in the book.

Ehsan M. Entezar
Modesto, California
26 March, 2010

INTRODUCTION

Afghanistan is a multilingual society, with Dari and Pashto being the two dominant languages. Of these two, Dari is the interethnic language by which most, if not all, of the native speakers of other languages (Pashto, Uzbeki, Turkmeni, Pashai, Baluchi, and others) can communicate with each other. Pashto is generally spoken in the south and east, but it is also spoken in the north and western regions of the country. Dari is spoken natively in the capital Kabul, northern, central, and the western parts of Afghanistan as well as in Gardez and Jelalabad in the southeast and east respectively. Uzbeki is the native language of the Uzbek people in the northwest, but it is also spoken in some other northern regions. Turkmeni is mostly spoken in the northwest close to the border of Turkmenistan. Baluchi is spoken in the southwest, and Pashai in Nuristan, in eastern Afghanistan.

The Persian Language

The Persian language is spoken by about a hundred million people. Its native speakers live in Iran, Afghanistan, Tajikistan, and Uzbekistan. There are three major dialects of Persian: Farsi, Tajiki, and Dari. Farsi is spoken in Iran, Tajiki in Tajikistan and Uzbekistan, and Dari in Afghanistan. Most Afghans call Dari "Farsi" but Dari is the official name for it. Within Afghanistan, there are different regional dialects of Dari. The major dialects of Dari are Kabuli, Hazaragi, (central Afghanistan), Herati (Herat), and Badakhshi spoken in Badakhshan, south of the Tajikistan border. These dialects differ in pronunciation, vocabulary, and grammar. While these Dari dialects differ in grammar and vocabulary, the differences in pronunciation are more acute. Among these dialects, Hazargi is more different from Kabuli and other dialects of Dari. Nevertheless, they are all dialects of Dari, and by definition mutually intelligible. The dialect used in this book is Kabuli, spoken in Kabul, where the author was born and raised.

Diglossia

The phenomenon of switching language forms is called diglossia, according to which, the speaker moves between more and less formal language, depending on the target audience and the social situation. Diglossia is characteristic of societies where literacy is very low. In the Arab world, like Afghanistan, where diglossia is also common, the written language is considered sacred and more prestigious than the spoken, because the Koran is in Arabic. Since language changes and writing relatively stays the same, after the passage of time, the gap between the two widens to the point that they become mutually unintelligible.

Diglossia has advantages and disadvantages. One advantage is that, in the presence of so many different dialects, the written language is the only means whereby educated/literate people can communicate. This is the case in countries where Arabic and Persian are spoken. In the Arab world, where there are many different dialects, Modern Standard Arabic(MSA), is the only way for the Saudis, Lebanese, Iraqis, Egyptians, Syrians, and other native speakers, who speak different dialects of Arabic, to communicate. In other words, these Arabs can understand MSA, the language of print and electronic media, if they are literate. Similarly, in Iran, Afghanistan, Tajikistan, and Uzbekistan, where people speak different dialects of Persian, the written language is the best means of communication.

Diglossia, however, has more disadvantages. One involves literacy. For a non-literate person to become literate, he/she has to learn a new system, a different form of language to comprehend the language used in radio and television, and formal speeches. Most non-literate Afghans don't understand the news and formal speeches since they are presented in the form of the written language.

Another problem of diglossia is related to learning Dari as a foreign language. While a native speaker of Dari has to learn one new system to become literate, a non-native speaker of Dari has to learn two. Obviously, this would be too much of a burden, as it would involve a simultaneous mastery of two systems: spoken and written. Therefore, for a person who is primarily interested in carrying on a conversation with ordinary Afghans, it is better to initially concentrate only on learning the spoken language. Once he has learned the spoken form, he can then proceed and learn the written language.

Still another disadvantage of diglossia in societies such as Afghanistan is that, there is a tendency on the part of the educated to teach the written form to foreigners. For example, when I wrote my first Dari book for the U.S. Peace Corps in 1964, some professors at Kabul University where I was teaching, wanted to know why the book was not in formal, literary or *adabi* Dari. Their reaction was based on the fact that the spoken language is considered "the street language" even though they themselves use it at home and in the work placc.

For the same reason, when Afghans want to speak with foreigners, or talk on the radio/television, they usually switch to the "bookish" or written version of Dari. Even tutors tend to teach bookish Dari to foreigners. Sometimes, Afghans "correct" foreigners and encourage them to speak bookish Dari. This explains the use of bookish expressions in some commercially available phrase books. Uneducated Afghans, too, when talking to foreigners, use bookish words. For example, instead of saying /ma/ "I" they say /man/, the more formal form.

Diglossia has implications for the Afghan government and the international community, when it comes to communicating with the public. To educate and inform the masses, the electronic media, radio, and television must use the spoken form of Dari since the majority (more than 80 percent) of Afghans are non-literate. Dialogue and round table forums are probably most effective because the spoken language is usually used. In short, to reach more listeners and viewers, radio and televison programs need to make more use of spoken Dari.

Different Systems

Apart from the alphabet, spoken and written Dari differ in pronunciation, vocabulary, and, syntax. Phonologically, the equivalent of the first sound in the English word "hat" does not exist in the spoken language. Additionally, some Arabic letters that used to be pronounced in loan words from Arabic, have no equivalents in spoken Dari: /ayn/, /towy/, /zowy/, /swaat/, and /dwaat/. These Arabic letters, however, are sometimes pronounced in written Dari, especially by the cleric, and those who have studied Arabic.

Differences in vocabulary, however, are much more stark and numerous. Some words are slightly similar; others are completely different, and still others that have no equivalents in spoken Dari at all. In the following pairs, where the first is written, and the second spoken, there is some similarity between the two: / khwaahad/: /khaat/ "will/might," /man/: /ma/ "I," /khwaahar/: /khwaar/ "sister,";/chahaar/: /chaar/ "four." Some words are completely different between the two: /nokhost: /awal/ "first"; /andeysha/: /fekr/ "thought"; / mobaareza/: / jang/ "fight"; /tahawol/: /taghir/ "change"; /saa.el/: /gadaayigar/, /mostakhdem/: /nowkar/ "servant." Finally, for some written words there are no spoken words: /laaek/ "secular," /nezaam/ "stucture/organization," /anaasor/ "elements," / ebtekaar/ "innovation," /zawaabit/ "principles, /eytelaaf/ "coalition." The vocabulary in the last category is numerous, involving thousands of words related to concepts in the social and natural sciences. To understand such terminology, one has to go to school and /or be functionally literate to have read books. This is understandable. Words express ideas and concepts, and when an individual is unfamiliar with a concept, he/she should not be expected to know the word or expression for it.

Language is a means of communication and a crucial tool for development. In Afghanistan, however, it is more a means of self-advancement, showoff, and domination[1]. Hence the use of "flowery" language, and so much sensitivity and fuss about Pashto and Dari words in the Afghan Press and even Parliament.

In grammar too, there are some differences between written and spoken Dari though not as stark and numerous. These variations involve tense and time, subject-verb agreement, the interrogative, and several others. In written Dari, the word /khwaahad/ is used to express future tense. Thus, /man baraayash khwaahad goftam/ means "I will tell him/her." In spoken Dari, however, the same meaning is expressed as /ma baresh meygom/. The written word /khwaahad / is pronounced /khaat/, and it is used in the sense of "might," or "may" rather than future tense. In other words, it is a modal not a marker of future tense. In fact, as it will be made clear in chapter 2, neither written nor spoken Dari has future tense. Dari, written or spoken, has only past and non-past tenses.

Another grammatical difference between written and spoken Dari has to do with subject-verb agreement in number. Thus, in /bachahaa aamadand/ "The boys came," the verb /aamadand/ has the suffix /-and/ "they" whereas in the spoken, it is /bachaa aamad/ without the suffix. This is especially the case when the subject is inanimate. For example, in /meyzaa dar senf astand/ "The desks are in the classroom," is written form, but /meyzaa da senf-as/ in speech. Essentially then, there is no subject-verb agreement in number in the third person plural in spoken Dari.

Yet another grammatical difference between writing and speech has to do with the interrogative. To form a question in written Dari, the word /aayaa/ "whether/ if" is added to the beginning of a declarative to form a yes/no question. But in speaking, the sentence is pronounced with a rising intonation. Thus, one writes /aayaa bachahaa khaana raftand? / "Did the boys go home?" In the spoken form, on the other hand, only a rising intonation is sufficient.

It is worth noting that vocabulary variations between the two forms of Dari are major problems not just for the non-literate Afghans, but also for native speakers of English, learning to speak Dari. More specifically, it is the nouns because they are so numerous, and they change when new words enter the language.

Grammar

The word "grammar" is defined differently in linguistics than in popular usage. For the purposes of this study, grammar is used in the sense of phonology,

---

[1]   For more information on language sensivity and the related problems in Afghanistan, see *Afghanistan 101: Understanding Afghan Culture* pages 81-92.

morphology, and syntax. Phonology deals with the description of consonants, vowels, and semivowels, as well as stress (loudness), juncture (pause), intonation (pitch or tone). Morphology involves word formation. Finally, syntax is about the arrangement of words to make phrases and clauses . . .

The grammatical analysis of spoken Dari provided here is based to a large extent on Generative-Transformational linguistics. According to this theory, every language has a surface structure and a deep structure, and there are rules of formation (deep structure), and rules of transformation (surface structure). The former provides the basic or kernel sentence types, and the latter complex and compound sentences. For example, "Someone is painting the room," is the deep structure of "The room is being painted (by someone)." "Swimming pool," is the surface structure of "The pool is for swimming." Similarly, "The swimming pool is nice," is a complex sentence derived from embedding "The pool is for swimming," into "The pool is nice."

Phonemic Transcription

Phonemic transcription should not be confused with orthography and transliteration. Orthography refers to the art of writing words with proper letters according to the standard of usage.[2] More accurately, orthography refers to a writing system that employs characters to represent the spoken language. In an alphabetic writing system, the characters are letters as in English, Dari, and most other languages. In syllabic writing systems such as Japanese, the characters used represent syllables, while in idiographic writing systems such as Chinese, characters represent ideas rather than sounds or syllables.

Transliteration is to represent or spell in the characters of another alphabet. [3] Usually this process involves writing foreign words in a given orthography. For example, the English word "Koran" is a transliteration from Arabic. "Afghanistan" is another. It is important to keep in mind that the sounds of loan words must fit the phonological system, and orthography of the borrowing or target languages. In the above examples, the letter "K" does not represent the Arabic sound. Rather it is the closest sound (phoneme) in English. Sometimes the phonemes of another language are transliterated with two letters, for which there is one in the source language. Thus "gh" in the transliteration of "Afghanistan" is represented by one letter in Dari. Here too, since the closest English sound is /g/, it is pronounced as such, not as how "gh" is actually pronounced in Dari.

---

[2]   Merrium Webster's Collegiate Dictionary, 877.

[3]   Ibid, 1329.

What is then a phonemic transcription and why it is used in this book? In a phonemic transcription, phonemes are presented in such a way that, there is one-to-one correspondence between the speech sounds and characters (symbols). Phonemes are significant speech sounds that do not have any meaning of their own, but they can change the meaning of words. For example, /p/ and /b/ are two different phonemes in English because "pet" and "bet" are two different words. In Dari too, /paam/ and /baam/ are two different words because the former means "flat" and the latter "roof."

In a phonemic transcription, each phoneme is represented by only one symbol. For example, the sound /p/ is always represented by the English letter "p." This rule is followed for the most part with a few exceptions (see Pronunciation Guide). The exceptions involve sounds for which the English alphabet has no single letters. The Dari sounds that fall into this category are transliterated as "gh," and "kh," "zh," "ch," and "sh." Of these, the last three phonemes are also part of the English language phonological system: /zh/ in "vision," /ch/ in "chair," and /sh/ in "she." Unlike Dari orthography, English does not have single letters to represent these sounds.

In the case of vowels too, English orthography does not have single letters for long vowels. They include the vowels in the words, "see," "steak," "boots," "boat," "bought," and "sight." Dari equivalents of these long vowels and diphthongs are represented in this book as /i/, /ey/, /u/, /ow/, and /aay/ respectively. It is worth noting that in the phonemic transcription used in this book, utterances, words, phrases, and sentencesare written between slanted lines (//). Thus /khaana/ means "house, home, or room."

A phonemic transcription is used when a language has no writing system, or when a new writing system is adopted. For example, Pashai, spoken in eastern Afghanistan, does not have a writing system. To devise a writing system, a phonemic transcription would be used. In the 1920s, Turkey used a phonemic transcription to change its writing system from Arabic to Latin. And since, in such a transcription, there is one-to-one correspondence between speech sounds (phonemes) and letters (graphemes) written and spoken Turkish are the same. In other words, you write what you say and say what you write in Turkish. This one-to-one correspondence is referred as "fit" in linguistics. Initially, when a writing system is devised for an unwritten language, the fit is typically good. However, since speech changes and writing remains relatively the same, the fit gets worse and worse through the passage of time. Similarly, to teach spoken Dari to native speakers of English, a phonemic transcription is also used so the learner can concentrate on learning one system instead of two systems (spoken and written).

The supra-segmental phonemes-stress, juncture, and pitch—are not marked in this book due to lack of symbols in the keyboard. The exception being primary stress when discussing stress in Dari. As in a dictionary, /'/ is used for primary stress. Compare /'rafteym/ "We went," with /raf'teym/ "We have gone." Falling and rising intonations are marked at the end of an utterance as a period (.) and a question mark (?) respectively. The reader is advised to have a native speaker pronounce words and sentences used in the grammar and word phrase portions of the book, and mark word stress.

Lingua Franca

Dari is the *lingua franca* of Afghanistan. Most non-native Dari speakers can communicate with each other in Dari. This is because it has been the language of commerce and business in the country for centuries. This raises an important question of the two dominant languages of Afghanistan: which one should a foreigner learn? If a Westerner is going to be assigned in a Pashto-speaking region of the country, he/she would be better off to learn Pashto. If, on the other hand, he does not know where his assignment is, he/she would be better off learning Dari. Another factor that the learner needs to consider is that, since Pashto is a much harder language to learn, its mastery takes much longer. Unlike Dari and English, for example, Pashto has gender and case. In gender, the verb has different endings depending on whether the subject is feminine or masculine. Thus /karim laal./ means "Karim went." but /Halima laala/ means "Halima went." Note the feminine marker {-a} suffixed to the verb. Similarly, Pashto has two personal pronouns for the first person singular: /ze/ and /maa/. The former is used when the verb is in the non-past while the latter is employed when the verb is in the past and transitive. Hence /ze waayom/ means "I say/tell," but / maa wowayel. / means "I said." In phonology too, apart from the sounds /kh/ and /gh/ which also exist in Dari, Pashto has additional speech sounds such as /ts/, /dz/, and others that do not exist in English, and they are very difficult for a native speaker of English. Thus, a native speaker of English must take into consideration not just the location of assignment/deployment in Afghanistan, but also the complexity of the Pashto language in making a decision on whether to learn Dari or Pashto.

Language and Culture

Language and culture are closely related, as is well presented in Robert Hall's book on culture entitled *The Silent Language*. This close relationship between the two is clearly visible in translation of words, proverbs, poetry, and jokes. Dari, for example, has several words for rice dishes depending on how it is cooked and what ingredients are used. While this is an indication that rice is very important in Afghan culture, it causes problems of translation. Since English does not have words for these varieties of rice, a translator has no choice but to describe each variety using phrases. For example, *qaabeli* is a dish consisting of rice, raisins, carrots and meat.

It is not just translation of single words that makes the task challenging. The English sentence, "It was a homerun." cannot be translated in Dari word-for-word as doing so does not make sense. To provide a free translation, the translator must be familiar with American culture, namely familiarity with sports in America. The use of "homerun" in contexts other than sports means "success," and not "running home." Thus, the above English expression has to be translated into Dari as" It was a success."

The same is true when it comes to the translation of idioms, proverbs, and sayings. In an idiom, its meaning is not the sum of the individual words. Thus, "to kick the bucket" in English means "to die." "Kicking the bucket" in Dari only means hitting a bucket with one's leg. Translating jokes is even more problematic. I remember when I came to the United States in the 1960s, my roommate would laugh at Johnny Carson's shows, but not me. I did not think most of what he said was funny at all. This is because I was ignorant about American culture, not to mention my low proficiency in the English language. That is why it is said that understanding jokes is the highest stage of learning a foreign language. Thus, mastery of a language also calls for understanding the culture of the people who speak it.

For this reason, in the Phrase book section of this book, "Cultural Notes" have been added to help the reader understand, and properly use Dari in the Afghan cultural context. Effective communication in a second/foreign language also calls for an understanding of the culture of the people who speak it. Since Afghan and American cultures are 180 degrees different from each other, the reader is advised to refer to *Afghanistan 101: Understanding Afghan Culture* (2008), the first attempt to analyze Afghan culture systematically.

Language and Communication

Language is a means of communication and includes both *usage* and *use*. Usage refers to the formation of words, phrases, and clauses along with their meanings. To put differently, usage has to do with language structure or grammar. Language use, on the other hand, relates to communication, what happens when the words and sentences actually occur as how people speak and write. This dimension of language involves "the attitudes and behavior of the speaker and the listener." At the speaker's end, language can express attitudes and emotions; at the receiving end, language can control or influence the actions and attitudes of the hearer. Essentially, words and sentences can take on meanings and functions that go beyond or differ from what only the utterances mean.

A clear example can be seen in the English utterance, "You are wearing a blue shirt," which may be a compliment, an insult, a suggestion to change, a warning to beware criticism, an expression of the speaker's taste or preference, and many other possibilities, depending on the situation, and the knowledge of the speaker and the hearer.

These functions of language are often described as *speech acts*, meaning what we actually **do** with language. Speech acts are aspects of communication, not necessarily of language usage or structure.

This *Dari Grammar and Phrase book* deals with both language usage and language use. The grammar part is communication-oriented, using concepts mostly needed in communication, making it, as much as possible, a communicative grammar of Dari. In addition, usage and cultural notes help the reader understand how the linguistic material functions in real communication.

Book and Chapter Organization

There are two parts to *Dari Grammar and Phrase book*. Part 1, grammar consists of six chapters: phonology (1), the verb phrase (2), the noun phrase (3), the adjectival phrase (4), adverbs and prepositions (5), and clauses (6). In phonology, the formation and arrangement of Dari phonemes are discussed. More specifically, this chapter describes consonants, vowels and semivowels, as well as stress, juncture and pitch in the language. It also points out problems a native speaker of English might encounter in the mastery of Dari phonology and how to cope with them.

Each chapter begins with a summary of new concepts. This is followed by analysis of the concepts by providing the necessary examples and illustrations. Then comes the chapter summary. The chapter ends with some exercises on the topics discussed. The purpose of the exercises is to provide the reader with an additional learning opportunity, and to see if he or she has digested the material presented in the chapter.

Part 2, Phrase book, consists of language functions and topics. The former discusses briefly how Dari is used to ask / give information, agree/disagree, persuade/dissuade, give commands, and make suggestions, and so on. The topics include shopping, food, health, security, education, transportation, food, security, and climate, and so on. Each topic begins with a dialogue, providing the relevant structures. This is followed by a list of the appropriate vocabulary as nouns, verbs, and adjectives. The Phrase book also includes important cultural notes and proverbs related to a particular topic. In shopping, for example, the reader is informed about the importance of bargaining in Afghan society.

Dari Grammar and Phrase Book ends with three appendixes. In Appendix A, days of the week and months of the year are listed. Numerals (cardinal and ordinal numbers along with their superlative forms) are listed in Appendix B. Finally, Appendix C provides information about Afghan names. Here, the origin, meaning and makeup of Afghan names are provided.

PART 1

Grammar

1

Phonology

Phonology is the subfield of linguistics involving the structure and systematic patterning of speech sounds. More specifically, it refers to a description of the sounds of a particular language (consonants, vowels, semivowels and so on), and the rules governing the distribution of those sounds.

As in any language, describing the phonological system of Dari firstly involves identifying its phonemes. Phonemes are speech sounds that do not have any meaning of their own but they can change the meaning of words. Thus, /t/ and /d/ are different phonemes in English because "ba**t**" and "ba**d**" are two different words. Phonemes are segmental (consonants, vowels, and semivowels), and supra-segmental (pitch, juncture and stress).

Consonants

The consonants of a language are classified on the basis of point of articulation, manner of articulation, and voicing. Point of articulation involves what organs of speech touch each other and where in the mouth the sound is produced. For example, in the pronunciation of /b/, the two lips touch. Manner of articulation has to do with what happens to the air streams on its way out. The difference between /t/ and /s/, for example, is that in the former, the air is stopped completely whereas in the latter it is not. Finally, voicing involves vibration of the vocal cords. For instance, /t/ and /d/ only differ in voicing. In the production of /d/, the vocal cords vibrate (the phoneme is voiced) but in producing /t/ they do not (the phoneme is voiceless). Otherwise, in terms of point and manner of articulation, they are identical.

Dari consonants consist of stops, fricatives, affricates, nasals, liquids, and glides.

Stops are sounds during the production of which the air stream is stopped completely. Dari has seven stops namely: /p/, /b/, /t/, /d/, //k/,/g/, and /q/. (See Pronunciation Guide). Four of the stops, /p/, /t/, /k/ and /q/ are voiceless. Three of them, /b/, /d/and /g/ are voiced. The phonemes /p/, /b/, /k/, and /g/ are almost identical to their counterparts in English. However, Dari /t/ and /d/ are slightly different. In Dari, /t/ and /d/ are made with the tip of the tongue touching the upper teeth (dental). It is important to note, however, that this difference does not lead to misunderstanding. Not making these two sounds this way only causes an accent. Most Dari speakers have an accent when speaking English because, among other things, they use a dental instead of an alveolar pronunciation. Among the Dari stops, /q/ is problematic for native speakers of English as this sound does not exist in English. The sound /q/ is made further back in the mouth than /k/. The back of the tongue touches the back of the throat. Substituting /q/ for /k/ or vice versa in Dari changes the meaning of a word. For example, /qaar/ means "anger" and /kaar/ means "work." Working with minimal pairs such as this, a good teacher who is a native speaker of Dari, could systematically help the learner the recognition and production of this sound. A minimal pair is two words that differ only in one respect as /kaar/ and /qaar/. For such a practice, /q/ and /k/ need to be contrasted not just in the initial position, but also in the middle and final position of words.

Dari has seven fricative consonants. In the production of fricatives, the air stream on its way out is not stopped completely but there is enough constriction of the air to produce friction. Dari has seven fricatives, four voiceless and three voiced. The voiceless ones are /f/, /s/, /kh/ and /sh/, and the voiced ones are /z/, /zh/ and /gh/. Among the Dari fricatives, /kh/ /gh/ have no equivalents in English, making them problematic for its speakers learning Dari. These sounds have almost the same point of articulation as /q/. The difference is in manner of articulation, in that the air stream is not completely stopped as is the case with /q/. Dari /kh/ is in the German word for "night." The sound /gh/ is made when one gargles. It is like the German or French "r." There is a tendency on the part of native speakers of English to use the closest sounds in their language. They use /h/ or /k/ for /kh/ and /g/ for /gh/. Doing so of course leads to misunderstanding because /kaar/ means "work" and /khaar/ means "thorn." Similarly, /ghala/ means "grain" and /gala/ means "herd." Here too, with the help of a native speaker and by using minimal pairs, the learner can recognize and produce these problematic sounds.

Another class of consonants is the affricates. Affricates are a combination of two sounds: a stop followed by a fricative. For example, combining /t/ and /

sh/ produces /ch/. Similarly, /d/ and /zh/ produce /j/. The Dari affricates /ch/ and /j/ also exist in English: /ch/ as in "**ch**air" and /j/ as in "**j**ust." Therefore, production and recognition of these sounds should not be problematic.

Nasal sounds are those during the production of which the air stream goes through the nose (nasal) instead of the mouth (oral). Dari has two nasals: /m/ and /n/. They are almost identical to their counterparts in English. Dari does not, however, have the last sound in the English word "sing." Compare "sin" and "sing."

The liquids consonants in Dari are /r/ and /l/. Liquids are those speech sounds during the production of which the air stream flows easily. They share properties of both vowels and consonants. Like consonants, the tongue is raised toward the alveolar ridge, and like vowels the air stream flows without friction. Dari liquids are slightly different from their counterparts in English. Dari /r/ is a flap or trill depending on its position in the word whereas the English /r/ is retroflex, in that the tip of the tongue is slightly rolled back. But this difference is not significant and does not lead to misunderstanding. The Dari /l/ is almost identical to its counterpart in English.

Glides (/y/ and /w/) have vowel-like articulations that precede and follow true vowels. Glides /y/ and /w/ have the same articulations as the vowel in the word "beat" and "boot" respectively. In the initial position, they function like consonants, but in the medial and final, they function like vowels. Dari and English glides are almost identical and hence cause no misunderstanding or accent for that matter: /y/ as in "**y**es" and /w/ as in "**w**in."

Vowels

As in all languages, Dari and English vowels can be classified on the basis of the position of the tongue (front, center and back) and the jaw (high, mid, and low).

For example, note the following English words:

	Front	Back
High	beat	Boot
Low	bat	Bought

In addition, in Dari, as in many languages, there are short and long vowels. To give an English example, the vowel in "bit" is short and the one in "beat" is long.

In Dari, there are four short and four long vowels. The short vowels are /e/, /o/, / a/, and /aa/. Among these, /e/ and /o/ are high and /a/ and /aa/ are low.

	Front	Back
High	**/e/ as in /dest/ "hand"**	**/o/ as in /goft/ "said"**
Low	/a as in /bad/ "bad"	/aa/ as in /baad/ "wind"

The long vowels are /i/, /u/, /ow/, and /ay/: the first two of which are high, and the last two low and diphthongized. /u/ and /ow/ are back.

	Front	Back
High	/i/ as in /shir/ "milk"	/u/ as in /but/ "shoe"
Low	/ow/ as in /zowr/ "force/power"	/ay/ as in /chaay/ "tea"

> Among these vowels, /o/ is not problematic since it is almost like the English vowel in "put." Dari /e/ is somewhere between the vowels in "bit" and "bet" in English. Still it is not so much of a problem for native speakers of English. Dari /a/ and /aa/ are completely different vowel sounds, as can be seen in the different words, /shar/ "evil" and /shaar/ "city or town." Dari /a/ is close to but not identical to the vowel in the English word "bat," and /aa/ is close to the vowel in the word "bought."

Again exercises with minimal pairs can help in the recognition and production of these problematic vowels. Long vowels are not problematic because they also occur in English.

Stress and Intonation

Pitch, juncture, and stress are supra-segmental phonemes. Pitch is tone (high or low) which is significant at the sentence level. In both English and Dari, a sentence with a rising intonation is an interrogative, whereas a sentence with a falling intonation is a declarative. In some languages such as Chinese, tone is significant at the word level, but not in Dari or English.

Stress, on the other hand, means loudness and is significant in both languages at the word level.

The English word, "import" could be a noun or a verb depending on whether the primary stress falls on the first or the second syllable. In Dari too, the word /mardom/ could either mean "people" or "Oh, people" depending on which syllable the primary stress is placed. As another example, /rafteym/ means "We went," or "we have gone". If the primary stress is on the first syllable, it is the former and if it is on the second, it is the latter. In Dari, primary stress falls on the last syllable of nouns and first syllable of verbs. In English, on the other

---

26

hand, primary stress can fall on almost any syllable except nouns where it falls on the penultimate syllable. This difference can cause problems of accent when native speakers of English speak Dari. "Bagram", the U.S. military base north of Kabul, is a good example. Americans tend to stress the first syllable instead of the second. I remember clearly when I was in the States the first time. I called my friend Philips. I told the operator I wanted to speak with Philips placing the primary stress on the second syllable "Philips." She said "Who?" I repeated the word putting the primary stress on the second syllable. Finally, she said "You mean "Philips!" placing the primary stress on "Phil." This is understandable since stress is different in Dari and English. Misplacing the primary stress can cause misunderstanding, especially on the phone when the context is missing. As it has been pointed out, unless it is necessary to explain a grammatical feature, stress is not marked in this book.

Juncture or pause is also significant in both languages. It occurs between words, phrases, clauses, and at the end of sentences. For example, in English, it makes a difference in meaning whether there is a pause before or after the letter "n" in "a name." The result is either "a name" or "an aim." In Dari too, a pause, in /shalghammeykhora/, before /gham/ means "The cripple is worried," and after it, it means "He eats turnips."

Stress, pitch, and juncture combine to provide intonation patterns on the clause/sentence level. Thus a falling intonation signals a declarative sentence while a rising one means an interrogative in both Dari and English.

Intonation is also significant at the phrase or sentence level. In general, a falling tone expresses certainty, completeness, and independence while a rising tone does the opposite. Throughout this book, and in the following examples, a period (.) indicates a falling tone while a question mark (?) symbolizes a rising tone at the end of sentences, and a comma (,) at the end of phrases. In the following the key words are highlighted.

Examples:

1.	/ma **meyrom**./ "I'm leaving."	Falling
2.	/**do baja**-s./ "It's two o'clock."	Falling
3.	/emrowz awaa **sard**-as./ "It's cold today"	Falling
4.	/**meyra**? / "Is s/he going?"	Rising
5.	/**do baja**-s?/	Rising
6.	/karim, najib, **maar**i wa **ma** meyreym/ "Karim, Najib, Mary and I are leaving."	Rising and Falling
7.	/**cheraa** miri/ "Why are you going?"	Falling

Note that in sentence (6), there is a rising tone after Karim, Najib and Mary and a falling tone at the end of the sentence, and in (7) the sentence has a falling tone even though it is a question.

Syllable Types

A syllable has a peak and margin (beginning and ending). Vowels make the peak of syllables while consonants and semivowels their margins. The margins can consist of one or more than one consonant. Specifying the types of margins of a syllable provides the syllable types.

Let us look at the following examples to understand the nature of syllable in Dari.

Type 1.   V /i/ "this," /u/ "he/she" and /aa/ "yes"

Type 2.   CV /ma/ "I," /tu/ "you," /taa/ "until, to"

Type 3.   VC /aan/ "yes," /aash/ "noodle soup"

Type 4.   VCC /aard/ "flour," /mard/ "man," /asht/ "eight," /aft/ "seven"

Type 5.   CVC /kaar/ "work," /shaar/ "city," /khub/ "good"

Type 6.   CVCC /zard/ "yellow," /mard/ "man," /chand/ "how many/much," /dest/ "hand"

Type 7.   CCVC /pyaaz/ "onion,"/byaar/ "Bring," /khwaar/ "sister," /swaar/ "rider"

As the above syllable types indicate, Dari does not allow three consonant clusters in the initial, medial, or final position. This explains why a vowel is inserted in such words as "Afghanistan" (Afghan+stan) to prevent a three consonant cluster of /nst/. Additionally, Dari clusters consist of only two consonants, and in the initial position, the second consonant can only be either /y/ or /w/ (7). A further restriction in Dari clusters is that, in the final position, fricatives /s/ and /sh/ cannot be followed by a voiced stop such as /d/, /b/, and /g/ due to the process of assimilation. In other words, a voiceless fricative cannot by followed by voiced stop as the latter has to assimilate with the former. Thus final clusters such as /asp/, /ast/, /ask/, /asht/, /ashk/ are possible Dari words but not / asb/, /asd/, /asg/, /ashb//ashd/, and /ashg/.

In English, on the other hand, clusters can consist of two or three consoanats. The word "stop," for example, has two consnants (CCVC) while "strike" has a three-consonant cluster (CCCVC). That is why, Afghans learning English tend to insert a vowel before the initial clusters, or add a vowel in between.

Thus, the English word "student" is usually pronounced as either "**e**student" or "student." For native speakers of English learning Dari, however, consonant clusters should not be problematic.

Chapter Summary

The segmental phonemes consist of consonants, vowels, and semivowels. The consonants include /p/, /b/, /t/. /d/, /k/, /g/, /q/, /f/, /s/, /z/, /sh/, /zh/ / kh/, /gh/, /ch/, /j/ /m/, /n/, /l/ and /r/. Dari vowels are /e/, /ey/, /u/, /o/, /a/, / aa/, /ow/, and /aay/ while the semivowels are /y/ and /w/.

The supra-segmental phonemes include stress, pitch, and juncture. In Dari, the primary stress falls on the last syllable of nouns and adjectives, and on the first syllable of verbs. There seems to be seven different types of syllables in the language. Dari does not allow three-consonant clusters in any position. Two-consonant clusters, however, occur in the language. In the intial position, the second consonant has to be either /y/ or /w/. The problematic sounds for native speakers of English are /kh/, /gh/ and /q/. In vowels, contrasting /a/ and /aa/ is problematic. Finally, in supra-segmental phonemes, placing the primary stress on the last syllable of nouns is a problem. These problems can be overcome with a tutor/native speaker of Dari, using minimal pairs.

Exercises

1. Provide the syllable types for the following Dari words. The first one is done for you.

Word	Syllable Type
/khaana/ "house/room."	CVCV
/amrika/ "America"	
/dari/ "Dari"	
/pashtow/ "Pashto"	
/naarenj/ "orange"	
/setaara/ "star"	
/angoshtaa/ "fingers"	
/gharib/ "poor"	
/syayi/ "blackness"	
/chaarmaghz/ "walnut"	

2. Using the Pronunciation Guide in the book, provide the phonemic transcription of the following English words.

Spelling	Phonemic Transcription
/jip/	Jeep
Chalk	/_____/
Shopkeeper	/_____/
scholar.	/_____/
Dictionary	/_____/
photograph.	/_____/
Pleasure	/_____/
clock.	/_____/
Succeed	/_____/
stutter	/_____/
Schedule	/_____/
Seattle	/_____/

3. Based on your knowledge of syllable types, which of the following are possible Dari words and which are not. Put (D) in front of the former and (X)before the latter.

X /sfaarat/

____/qomri/   ____/samaaroq/

____/gowsaala/   ____/chatri/

____/sangsaa/   ____/panstu/

____/baakhabari/   ____/dontwan/

____/shekambu/   ____/sanwechaa/

____/tokhomdaan/   ____/paakat/

____/staada/   ____/shams/

____/daftaraa/   ____/baaghaa/

____/jaayband/   ____/khandaqzaar/

____/teflnaaz/   ____/tashakor/

____/pyaada/   ____/syaayi/

2

The Verb Phrase

Introduction

Grammar as defined in this book, involves phonology, morphology, and syntax. The previous chapter dealt with phonology. This and subsequent chapters in Part 1 are about words: their meanings, formations, arrangements and functions. More specifically, this part has to do with verbs, nouns, adjectives, adverbs, and prepositions as well as phrases and clauses. We begin with the verb. However, to understand the nature of verbs, it is necessary to briefly discuss word formation.

Words and Morphemes

Morphology is the study of morphemes. Morphemes are the smallest meaningful units in a language. Morphological meanings are either lexical/dictionary or grammatical. For example, the English word "books" consists of two morphemes: {book} and {-s}. The former has a dictionary meaning while the latter has a grammatical meaning, namely the plural suffix. Thus nouns, verbs, adjectives, adverbs fall into the first, while prefixes, infixes and suffixes (inflections and derivations), and function words (prepositions, articles and so on) belong to the second category. To put differently, all words are morphemes but not all morphemes are words. In the above example, {book} is a word but the plural marker is not because the former occurs by itself, whereas the latter is attached.

Defining Words

Word classes are defined not just semantically, as in traditional grammars, but also on the basis of their form and function. For example, in traditional grammars, a noun is defined as the name of people, animals, and objects. Yet in "Seeing is believing," both "seeing" and "believing" are nouns but neither denotes people, animals, or objects. Therefore, in modern grammars, meaning is not the only criterion used in the identification of words; form and function of words are also important to identify them.

A native speaker can identify words without knowing their meaning. An example from "Bonguage" (an artificial language) will illustrate this. In "The Bong bonged the bongs bongly," a native speaker of English knows a good deal about this sentence without knowing the meaning of the words used. He knows that the action took place in a definite time in the past because of [-ed]; he also knows that the doer of the action was "The Bong" because of its position, and that it was a proper name because of the capital letter "B." He also understands that the receiver of the action was "the bongs," due to its position after the verbs, and that the receiver was more than one because of the suffix {-s} attached to it. Finally, a native speaker of English knows that the action was performed in a certain manner because of the suffix {-ly}. Thus a native speaker can understand a good deal about the words used in the above example from Bonguage, due to morphological and syntactic clues in the sentence without knowing the meaning of the individual words used. The following pages and chapters explain what such morphological and syntactic clues are in the Dari language.

Morphemes are classified into free/ bound, empty/full, and open/close categories. In the word "books," for example, {book} is a free morpheme while {-s]} is bound. In other words, free morphemes occur in isolation whereas bound morphemes do not. Morphemes can also be empty or full. A full morpheme has a lexical or dictionary meaning while an empty one only has grammatical meaning. Thus nouns, verbs, adjectives, and adverbs are full and function words (determiners, prepositions, and others) are empty. Finally, some morphemes are open (inclusive) while others are closed (exclusive). In an open class, new words can be added, but not in close classes. In general, nouns, verbs, and adjectives are inclusive whereas prepositions, determiners, and other function words are exclusive. In other words, full/free morphemes belong to the open class while empty and bound morphemes fall into the category of closed class. That is why members of an open class are much more numerous than those of a closed class. As it has been pointed out, all words are morphemes but not all morphemes are words. The English plural marker {-s} is a morpheme but not a word because it does not occur in isolation. In short, words are those morphemes that occur by themselves.

As it was pointed out, parts of speech are defined on the basis of three criteria: meaning, form, and function. The following examples illustrate the so-called parts of speech:

Noun	ketaab qimat-as/ "**The book** is expensive."
Adjective	ketaab **khub**-as/ "The book is **good**."
Verb	/karim **aamad**/ "Karim **came**."
Adverb	/karim **zud** aamad/ "Karim came **fast**."
Preposition	/karim **da** khaana-s/ "Karim is **at** home."
Determinative	/**i** ketaab khub-as/ "**This** book is good."
Subordinator	/goftom **ke** borow/ "I said **that** you go."
Coordinator	/karim **wa** jamila aamadan/ "Karim **and** Jamila came.

Inflections and Derivations

Indo-European languages are either inflected (markings on words) or word-order languages. It Dari is largely an inflected language while English is mostly a word-order language. In an inflected language, word order is not fixed. This is because the object of sentence has the inflection {-a} {-ra} depending on whether the noun ends in a consonant or a vowel. Thus, in the Dari sentence / u mara goft/ "He/she told me," /u/ is the subject, not because of its position in the sentence but because it does not have the object marker {-ra}. Thus, / u mara goft/ and /mara u goft/ are synonymous. This word can be moved to the object position and it would still be the subject of the sentence. Similarly, / mara/ "me" is the receiver (object) of the action because of the object marker, {-ra}. In English, on the other hand, position is significant. "Mary saw John," and "John saw Mary," are different because in one "Mary" is the doer of the action while in the other, "Mary" is the receiver (object). Thus, in a word-order language such as English, position is crucial, but not in an inflected language such as Dari, in which changing the position of words in a sentence has a different purpose: emphasis.

Inflections are regular and do not change the class of words. Derivatives, on the other hand, are irregular and usually change the class of words. The noun marker {-s} or {-es} in English is an inflection because it can occur with almost all nouns, but {un-} in "unhappy" is not; one cannot add it to all adjectives. We cannot say "unsad," for example. Similarly, adding the plural marker to a noun does not make it a verb, for example. However, the derivative {-ness} changes an adjective such as "happy" into a noun, "happiness." The same is the case with other inflections and derivatives.

Verb Inflections

Semantically, verbs denote actions, events, and processes while syntactically, they take certain inflections and derivations, function as predicate in clauses, and have dependents (modifiers). Compared to the other parts of speech, Dari verbs are the most important constituents in a clause, because they fill the predicate position, and provide the "message" or "complete thought." In English, for example, the phrase "had a good time" provides the message in "He had a good time." The subject "he" does not tell us much by itself without the predicate, "had a good time." In inflected languages such as Dari, the verb is even more important because it indicates not just the action, but also the subject (doer of action), and the object (receiver of action). It expresses "a complete thought." For example, the verb /nameykhoromesh/ "I don't eat it." Consists of five morphemes: {-na-} "not," {-mey-} present tense, {-khor-} "eat," {-om-} "I" and {-esh} "it." To express this meaning in English, five separate words must be used instead of one: "I do not want it." The above Dari utterance is a nonemphatic sentence since a separate subject and object pronoun is missing. Emphatic sentences require separate subjects and objects.

Dari verbs are inflected with person, tense, negation, participle, and others, as illustrated in the following table, using the verb "to go."

1	**Present/ non-past tense**	mey-	/u khaana **mey**ra/	"He/She/It goes home."
2	**Present stem**	-r-	/ma mey**r**om/	"I go."
3	**Subject** (suffix subject) pronoun)	-eym	/maa meyr**eym**/	"We go."
4	**Optative** (modality)	bo-	/baayad ma **bo**rom/	"I should go."
5	**Negative**	na-	/ma **na**meyrom/	"I don't go."
6	**Past participle** (present perfect)	Simple past+a	/u **raf'ta**/	"He/she/it has gone."
7	**Causative**	-aa-	/meyd**aa**nomesh/	"I make him run."
8	**Past stem**	goft-	/**gofto**mesh/	"I told him/her."
9	**Object** (suffix object pronoun)	-esh	/didom**esh**/	"I saw him/her/it."
10	**Past participle**	mey+simple past	/**mey**raft/	"He was going/used to go."

| 11 | Past Habitual | mey+simple past | /ma ar rowz **mey**khaandom/ | "I used to read everyday." |
| 12 | Imperative | bo- | /**borow**/ | "Go!" |

The linking verb (Be) has the following forms:

1	**Present stem**	-st-	/ma khaana-**st**om/	"I am home."
2	**Subject** (suffix subject)	-an	/waa khaana-st**an**/	"They are home."
3	**Past stem**	Bud	/u khaana **bud**/	"They were at home."
4	**Optative**	baash-	/baayad ma da khaana **baash**om/	"I should be home."
5	**Present habitual**	baash	/ma rowzaa-ye joma khaana/ **meybaash**om	"I am usually home."
6	**Imperative**	Baash	/khaana **baash**/	"Stay home."
7	**Future**	meybaash-	/aale da kaabol-astom, amaa basaal da amrikaa **meybaash**om/	"I am in Kabul now, but I'll be in America next year."
8	**Past habitual**	meybud-	/paarsaal rowzaa-ye joma da khaana **meybod**om/	"Last year I used to be home on Fridays."

Note that the imperative (6) and optative form (4) of /-as/ "being" is /baash / (6) and it does not take the present tense marker {-mey-} (1 and 2). When {-mey-} attached to /baasha/. It usually expresses habitual or future tense (5 and 7), the past form of both /as/ and /baasha/ is /bud/ or /bud/ (3 and 8) the and, when {mey-} is attached to the past stem, it expresses past habit, as is the case with other verbs.

Present and Past Stems

All Dari verbs, linking and others, have present and past stems. Stems are bound morphemes because they do not occur in isolation. Unlike English, Dari has no basic verb forms (the infinitive), from which to derive present, participle and past forms. For example, from the base form "to finish," "finishes," "finishing" and "finished" are derived. What is called "Masdar" (literally "source/

root" in Arabic) in traditional grammars, is not an infinitive in Dari since the present and past verb forms are not derived from it. This term is borrowed from Arabic in which it is indeed applicable, because the terms like masdar /kataba/ "to write" /kaateb/, uaktabu/ /maktub/ ketaab and other noun and verb forms are derived. In Dari, however, *masdar* is actually a gerund: a noun, from which only past verb forms are derived. A gerund is formed from the simple past stem for the third person singular, by adding the noun marker {-an}. For example, {raftan} "going" is formed from {raft} "He went." with the suffix {-an}. There is no formal relationship between /daadom/ "I gave." and /meytom/ "I give." as there is between "I finished." and "I finish." That is because /daadan/ is a past stem from which present stems are not derived. To figure out the stems, the inflections need to be extracted. In /meyrum/ "I go." {mey-} and {-om} are verb inflections and {-r-} is the present stem. Similarly, in /meyraftom/ "I was going." {mey-} and {-om} are the inflections and {-raft-} is the past stem.

Most present and past verb stems have very little in common. For example, in the present and past verb stems for "go," the only commonality is /r/. However, in /meytom/ "I give," and /daadom/ "I gave," the present and past stems are {-t-} and {daad-} respectively, where there is no commonality at all. In short, there is no connection between the present and past stems in Dari, just as there is no relationship between "go" and "went" in English. Therefore, they have to be memorized.

For the most part, there is nothing in common in the present verb stems but all past stems end either in /t/ or /d/. One can refer to them as T-Stems and D-Stems as the examples below illustrate:

Present Stem	Past Stem	T/D Stem
/mey**r**om/ "I go."	/**raft**om/ "I went."	T-Stem
/mey**gard**om/ "I walk/turn."	**gasht**om/ "I walked/turned."	T-Stem
/mey**showy**om/ "I wash."	/**shosht**om/ "I washed."	T-Stem
/mey**g**om/ "I say."	/**goft**om/ "I said."	T-Stem
/me**khaay**om/ "I want."	/**khaast**om/ "I wanted."	T-Stem
/mey**taan**om/ "I can."	/**taanest**om/ "I could."	T-Stem
/mey**faam**om/ "I know/understand."	/**faamid**om/ "I understood."	D-Stem
/mey**daw**om/ "I run."	/**dawid**om/ "I ran."	D-Stem
/mey**khar**om/ "I buy."	/**kharid**om/ "I bought."	D-Stem
/mey**aay**om/ "I come."	/**aamad**om/ "I came."	D-Stem
/mey**kon**om/ "I do."	/**kad**om/ "I did."	D-Stem
/mey**paal**om/ "I search/look."	/**paalid**om/ "I looked/searched."	D-Stem

/**ast**om/ "I am."	/**bod**om/ "I was."	D-Stem
/mey**baash**om/ "I am, usually"	/mey**bod**om/ "I used to be."	D-Stem

Free and Bound Pronouns

Dari has both free and bound pronouns as subjects and objects. Thus, in /ma goftom./ "I said." /ma/ and {-om} are respectively free and bound subject pronouns. Similarly, in /u mara goft/ "He/She told me." /mara/ is a free object pronoun. Free object pronouns always take the object marker {-a} or {-ra} depending on whether the noun or pronoun ends in a vowel or a consonant. Free pronouns are used in emphatic sentences while bound pronouns are attached to the verb. The difference between subject and object pronouns is that the former is obligatory but the latter is not. In other words, {-om} is required even if a free pronoun such as /ma/ "I" is present in the sentence. This is not so when object pronouns are involved. Here, one can either say /mara goft/ "He/She told me." or /goftem/. Free pronouns are discussed in the next chapter. Since bound pronouns are attached to verbs, they are dealt with here.

Both present and past verb stems are marked with person (subject/object) and number.

Subject Pronouns

	Singular	Plural
First person	/-om/ "I"	/-eym/ "we"
Second person	/-i/ "you" singular or familiar	/-eyn/ "you" plural or polite
Third person	/-a/ "he/she"	/-an/ "they"

Thus:

"Go":

First person./ mey**rom**/ "I go."   /mey**reym**/ "We go."

Second person / mey**ri**/ "You (familiar) go."   /mey**reyn**/ "You go."

Third person /mey**ra**/ "He/She/ It goes."   /mey**ran**/ "They go."

"Be":

First person /ast**om**/ "I am."   /ast**eym**/ "**We** are."

Second person /ast**i**/ "**You** (familiar) are."   /ast**eyn**/ "**You** are."

Third person / as/ "he/She/It"   /ast**an**/ "**They** are."

Note that in the third person singular, the suffix pronoun is zero.

Object Pronouns

	Singular	**Plural**
First person	/-e-m/ "me"	/-e-ma/ "us"
Second person	/-e-t/ "you" singular or familiar	/-e-aan/ "you" plural or polite
Third person	/-e-sh/ "him/her"	/-e-shaan/ "them"

Examples:

"Say/Tell"

I. Person /goftem/ "He/she told me."   /goftemaa/ "He/she told us."

II. Person /goftet/ "He/she told you (familiar)."   /goftetaan/ "He/she told **you**."

III. Person / goftesh/ "He/she told him/her."   /gofteshaan/ "He told them."

In the above examples, there are in fact, three morphemes: verb stem + izafa (connector) + pronoun. The connector, [-e], commonly referred to as Izafa, connects the modifier with the word modified. In the above examples, the Izafa is added to connect the verb stem with the suffixed pronoun. The presence of Izafa here can be understood better if its long and short forms are compared: /goftem/ is derived from /goft-e ma/ or /mara goft/ "He/she told me." As another example, /ketaab-**em**/ "my book" is derived from its emphatic, or long form /ketaab-e ma/ "my book." The Izafa also shows up in other contexts such as the possessive pronouns to be discussed in the next chapter.

Tense and Time

The prefix {mey-} indicates present or non-past tense when attached to the present verb stems, and past participle, or past habitual when attached to past stems. Spoken Dari does not have future tense. Neither does it have a present participle. Thus, /meyrom/ can either mean "I go," or "I am going," depending on the context. To express an action in progress, time words such as /aaley/ "now," /ami desti/ "right this moment," or /dey dey/ "continuously" are employed. Thus, /aale naan meykhoran/ or /dey dey naan meykhoran/ means "They are eating now." When {-mey} is used with past stems, it can mean continuation of an action or a past habit. For example, /meraftom/ can mean "I was going" or "I used to go."

Among the linking verbs /bodan/ (being) and /shodan/ (becoming), only /shodan/ takes the non-past inflection {mey-}. It is also important to note here that {mey-} is used only with the optative form of the verb of being as in /meybaashom/ where it means "usually." Thus, /rowzaa-e joma da khaana meybaashom/ means "I am usually home on Fridays," whereas /khaana-stom/ means "I am home (right now)."

The Negative

The negative prefix has two variations: **{na-}** and **{ney-}**. The prefix {na-} is used before concomitants and {ney-} before vowels. Thus the negative form of /astom/ "I am" is /**ney**stom/ but that of /meyrom / "I go." is /**na**meyrom/ "I don't go."

Examples:

Present	Past
/**na**meyrom/ "I don't go."	/**na**raftom/ "I didn't go."
/khaana **na**meybaashom/ "I am not usually home."	/khaana **na**bodom/ "I wasn't home."
/khaana **ney**stan / "They are not home."	/khaana **na**bodan/ "They were **not** home."

Present and Past Perfect

The present perfect is made from the past stem and stress changes. In other words, the simple past is converted into the present perfect, by shifting the primary stress /'/ from the first syllable to the second. Thus, /rafti/ means "You went," but /raft'i/ means "You have gone."

Examples:

Simple Past	Present Perfect	Past Perfect
First /raft**om** / "I went." /'rafte**ym**/ "We went."	/raft'**eym**/ "I have gone." /raft'**eym**/ "We have gone	/raft'a bod**om**/ "I had gone." /raft'a bod**eym**/ "We had gone."
Second /'rafti/ "You went." /'raft**eyn**/ "You (Pl.) went."	/raft'i/ "You have gone." /raft'**eyn**/	/raft'a bodi/" You had gone." /raft'a bod**eyn**/

Third /raft/ "He/She/It went." /'raftan/ "They went."	raft'**a**/" He/She/It has gone." /raft'**an**/ "They have gone."	/raft'a bud/ "He had gone." /raft'a bod**an**/" They had gone."

It is important to note that, the ending for the first person singular changes from {-om} to {-eym} in the present perfect. The third person plural forms are the same in the simple past and present perfect, except that the primary stress /'/ falls on the first syllable in the simple past /'raftom/ "I went," but in the second /raft'eym/ "I have gone." In the present perfect and past perfect, the third person singular ending in the simple past is zero, but {-a} in the present perfect and the past participle is made from the third person singular of the present perfect plus /bodan/ "being."

The Optative

Dari verbs are also inflected with what is called the optative, as it expresses option or modality. As the following examples illustrate, the optative is prefixed to the verb proper or a non-linking verb, when the sentence is: in the imperative (#1); when a modal is present (#2, #3 and #9), when the main verb is /khaastan/ "to want," or /delem meysha/ "I want" (#4 and #5), and when the main clause has a linking verb and an adjective (#7 and #8). Note also that in the negative, the optative is dropped (6) and sentences #2, #9 and #10 have synonymous constructions.

1. /**bo**row/ "Go."
2. /baayad (key) **bo**rom/ "I should go."
3. /kaashke paysara pas **be**ta/ "I hope he will return the money."
4. /meykhaayom ke **bo**rom/ "I want to go."
5. /delem meysha ke **bo**rom/ "I wish/ desire to go."
6. /narrow/ "Don't go."
7. /khub-as ke borom/ "It's better that I go."
8. /khub meysha ke borom/ "its better that I go."
9. /baayad-as ke borom/ "Is should go."
10. /baayad borom/ "I should go."
11. /baayad khaana baashom/ "I should be home."
12. /baayad kaar khalaas shawa/ "The work should be finished."

The optative has a completely different form with the linking verb /bodan/ "being" and /shodan/ "becoming." Thus:

Non-optative	Optative/Imperative
/khaana-**stom**/ "I'm home."	/baayad khaana **baashom**/ "I should be home."
/khaana-**sti**/ "You are home."	/khaana **baash**/ "Stay at home."
/khaana-**s**/ "He is home."	/baayad khaana **baasha**./ "He should be home."
kaar khalaas meysha/ "The work will finish."	/kaar baayad khalaas shawa/ "The work should be finished."

The negative of the optative form is also different with the verb of being and becoming. Unlike the verb proper, the negative is prefixed to the linking verb. Compare: /baasha/ "He/She/It should be/stay." and /**na**baasha/ "He/She/It should not be/stay." /khub meysha/ "It will be/become good." /khub nameysha/ "It won't be good." /baayad khub shawa/ "It should become good," and / baayad kharaab nasha/ "It should not become bad."

The Causative

The inflection {-aan-} is attached to the verb stem to cause to or make someone or something do something. It precedes the suffix pronouns (subject and object). The causative inflection also changes intransitive verbs into transitive. When the object is mentioned separately, the object pronoun is deleted. Thus, /saga meydawaanom/ "I run the dog." but not /saga meydawaanomesh/:

Examples:

/meydaw**aan**omesh/ "I **cause** him/her/it **to** run."
/meyfaam**aan**omesh/ "I **cause** him/her to learn/understand."
/meykhowr**aan**omesh/ "I **make** him/her/ it eat it."
/meysharm**aan**omesh/ "I **cause** him/her embarrassment."
/meylarz**aan**omet/ "I **make** you shake."

Transitive and Intransitive Verbs

As the following examples illustrate, Dari has both transitive and intransitive verbs. The former can be mono-transitive or di-transitive. A mono-transitive verb takes one object (#1, #2, and #5), while di-transitive ones take two (#3, #6, and #7). Almost all di-transitive verbs require the indirect object to be a prepositional phrase (#6). The verb /daadan/ "giving" may be the only di-transitive verb that can be used with or without a preposition (#3 and #7).

Most transitive verbs are mono-transitive. Additionally, with the verb /goftan/ "tell," the direct object always takes a preposition (#6). Finally, it is important to keep in mind that certain mono-transitive verbs require inanimate nouns as their objects; /shonidan/ "hearing" is such a verb (#8). Unlike English, in Dari, you don't hear people, birds, or animals and so on. Instead you hear a person's voice/lecture or a birds singing. Thus, it is ungrammatical to say /mara shonidi/ "Did you hear me?" This is another translation problem on television talk shows and conversations among some Afghan Americans.

Examples:

1. /naaan meykhorom/ "I'm eating (a meal)." . . .   Mono-transitive
2. /ketaaba khaandom/ "I read the book." . . .   Mono-transitive
3. /ketaaba mara daad/ "He gave me the book." . . .   Di-transitive
4. /khaana raftom/ "I went home." . . .   Intransitive
5. / raadeyowra shonidom/ "I heard the radio." . . .   Mono-transitive
6. /bar-e ma qesa goft./ "He told a story."   Di-transitive
7. /bar-e ma ketaab daad/ "He /She gave a book to me."   Di-transitive
8. /gap-e shomaara shonidom/ "I heard what you said."   Di-transitive

Simple and Compound Verbs

Another feature of Dari verbs is that, they are either simple or compound. Compound verbs are formed by combining a noun or an adjective with the present and past stems of **kadan/** "doing," /**zadan/** "hitting," and /**daadan/** "giving." As the following examples illustrate, the second word in the compound is inflected.

Noun+ {kadan} "do"	Compound Verb
/sayl/ "observation"	/sayl meykonom/ "I see/watch/ observe."
/waada/ "a promise"	/waada meykonom/ "I promise."
/jagra/ "bargaining"	/jagra meykonom/ "I bargain."
/emzaa/ "signature"	/emzaa meykonom/ "I sign."
/rang/ "color, paint"	/rang mekonom/ "I paint."
/andaaza/ "measurement"	/andaaza meykonom/ "I measure."
/kharch/ "expenditure"	/kharch meykonom/ "I spend."
/esaab/ "count/math"	/esaab meykonom/ "I count."

/zarb/ "multiplication"	/zarb meykonom/ "I multiply."
/khaw/ "sleep"	/khaw meykonom/ "I sleep."
/esteraa.at/ "rest"	/eteraa.at meykonom/ "I rest."
/fekr/ "thought"	/feker meykonom/ "I think."
/teylefun/ "telephone"	/teylefun mey konom/ "I call."
/kelek/ "click"	/kelek meykonom/ "I click."
/raajester/ "registration"	/raajester meykonom/ "I register."

Adjective + {kadan} "do"

/khosh/ "like/favorable"	/khosh meykonom/ "I choose."
/kharaab/ "bad"	/kharaab meykonom/ "I ruin/ destroy."
/nezdik/ "near"	/nezdik meykonom/ "I bring closer."
/aabaad/ "build"	/aabaad meykonom/ "I build."
/beydaar/ "awake"	/beydaar meykonomesh/ "I awaken him/her/it."
/paak/ "clean"	/paak meykonom/ "I clean."
/dur/ "remove/move/ far"	/dur meykonom/ "I move."

Noun + {zadan} "hit/strike"

/gap/ "talk"	/gap meyzanom/ "I talk/speak."
/daawaa/ "argument"	/daawaa meyzanom/ "I argue."
/chana/ "bargain"	/chana meyzanom/ "I bargain."
/laaf/ "boast"	/laaf meyzanom/ "I brag/ boast."
/chaal/ "trick"	/chaal meyzanom/ "I trick (someone)."
/shaana/ "shoulder"	/shaana meyzanom/ "I shoulder (someone physically)."
/chort/ "worry, think"	/chort meyzanom/ "I worry."

Noun+ {daadan} "give"

/dars/ "lesson"	/dars meytom/ "I teach."
/pas/ "back"	/pas myaayom/ "I return."
/aazaar/ "bother"	/aazaar meytom/ "I bother."
/jazaa/ "punishment"	/jazaa meytom/ "I punish."

/showr/ "stir/move"   /showr meytom/ "I stir/shake."
/aw/ "water"   /aw meytom/ "I water."
/fereyb/ "fool/trick"   /feryb meytom/ "I fool/trick."

Modals

Modals are a subclass of verbs. There are inflected and non-inflected modals (operators) in Dari. One inflected modal, which behaves like any verb, takes verb inflections and has present and past stems, is /taanestan/ "can/being able." With this modal, the verb does not have a tense as it is the past participle form of the verb. For example, in /khowrda meytaanum/ "I can eat," the second element, /meytaanum/ is the inflected modal.

Present	Past
/kowrda metaanom/ "I can eat."	/khowrda taanestom/ "I could eat."
/dida meytaanom/ "I can see."	/dida taanestom/ "I could see."
/aamada meytaanom/ "I can come."	/aamada taanestom/ "I could come."
/faamida meytaanom/ "I can	/faamida taanestom/ "I could." understand."
/gofta meytaanom/ "I can tell/say."	/gofta taanestom/ "I could tell/say."
/rafta meytaanom/ "I can go."	/rafta taanestom/ "I could go."
/shonida meytaanom/ "I can hear."	/shonida taanestom/ "I could hear."
/yaafta meytaanom/ "I can find."	/yaafta taanestom/ "I could find."

The non-inflected modals are /baayad/ "should," /momken/ "possible," /shaayad/ "may," and /khaat/ "might." With the exception of /khaat/ that only takes the negative inflection, these modals are not inflected. As it has been pointed out, the verb must be in the optative form in the present tense and {mey-} in the past, in affirmative clauses. In negative clauses, the optative {bo-} is dropped in the present tense, whereas in the past tense, the {mey-} remains. Thus:

Present	Past
/**baayad** borom/ "I should go."	/**baayad** meyraftom/ "I should have gone."
/**shaayad** borom/	/**shaayad** meraftom"
/**baayad** narom/ "I shouldn't go."	/**baayad** nameyraftom/ "I should not have gone."

/**nakhaat** borom/ "I might not go."	/**nakhaat** meyraftom/ "I might not have gone."
/**khaat** borom/ "I might go."	/**khaat** meyraftom/ "I might have gone."
/**momken** borom/ "I may go."	/**momken** meyraftom/ "I might have gone."
/**momken** narom/ "I may not go."	**momken** nameraftom/ "I might not have gone."
baayad baashom/ "should be/stay"	**baayad** meybodom/ "I should have."

The Verb Phrase

A verb phrase has a head or nucleus and modifiers or dependents. As the following examples illustrate, a verb can be modified by an adjective, an adverb, a noun, a noun phrase or a clause. As it will be clear in chapter 6, verb phrase is the most important constituent in a sentence as it determines the basic sentence type.

Examples:

/**teyz** merom/ "I'm going fast."	**Adverb**
/**khub** meysha/ "It will be good."	**Adjective**
/**ketaaba** gereftom./ "I took the book."	**Noun**
/**ketaab-e entezaara** kharidom/ "I bought Entezar's book."	**Noun Phrase**
/meykhaayom **ke khaana borom**/ "I want to go home."	**Noun Clause**

Chapter Summary

Verbs are defined not just on the basis of meaning. Their form and function are also critical in their identification. Dari verbs are inflected with tense, mood, aspect, negation, participle, causation, and subject and object pronouns. It is because of such inflections that a verb in Dari expresses a "complete thought." In this chapter, a distinction is made between words and morphemes.

Verbs are modified by adjectives, adverbs and nouns, noun phrases and clauses. Unlike English, Dari verbs have present and past stems. They can be transitive or intransitive. Transitive verbs in turn can be mono-transitive or di-transitive, linking or non-linking.

Tense in Dari is past and non-past (present-future), habitual and progressive. There is no present progressive or future tense but only past progressive. Dari also has present and past perfect tense.

The linking verb of being, /bodan/, has two forms: /as/ and /baasha/. The second form is used in the imperative, and in the presence of modals; /bash/ also expresses future and habitual action. The past form of both /as/ and /bash/ is /bud/ "was."

Modals are bound and free. The optative {bo-} expresses a kind of modality. When a sentence has one of the free modals such as {baayad}, {shaayad} or {momken}, the verb must be in the optative form. Also, when the main verb is {delem meysha} or {meykhaayom}, the verb in the dependent clause is in the optative form.

A compound verb is formed from a noun or an adjective by adding {kadan} "doing" {daadan} "to give" or /zadan/ "to hit" Finally, verb modifiers are adjectives, adverbs, nouns, noun phrases and noun clauses.

Exercises

1. Identify the verb stems in the following.

Verb	Stem
/meypaalom/	-paal-
/raftom/	_____
/nameygoftom/	_____
/nameygom/	_____
/meydawaanom/	_____
/zadesh/	_____
/meykhaanom/	_____
/astom/	_____
/nameybaashom/	_____
/bora/	_____
/meybaasha/	_____

2. In the following, identify the tense of each verb as to whether it is **past** or **non-past**.

Verbs	Tense
/kharidan/	past
/myaarom/	_____

46

/meyshaanom/ _____

/zad/ _____

/sayl kad/ _____

/khawaandeym _____

/byaar/ _____

/khaastom _____

/nameyga _____

/narafta _____

3. Identify the number of morphemes in the following:

Word	Number of Morphemes
/mefaama/	3
/nameygomesh/	_____
/afghaanestaan/	_____
/neystom/	_____
/bokhoreyn/	_____
/naamadan/.	_____
/khaali mekona/	_____
/pas daadom/	_____
/meygoftan/	_____
/borow/	_____
/nameybaashom/	_____

4. Translate the following sentences into Dari, using the following past and non-past stems:/-r-/ "to go,"/-daw-/ "to run," /shesht/, "sat," /khaan/ "to read," /-g-/ "to tell/say," /-khar-/ "to buy," /-zan-/ "to hit," /did/ "saw," /-ger-/ "to take," /-t-/ "to give."

English	Dari
I'm going.	/meyrom/
He will read it.	_____
Make him run.	_____
They saw it.	_____

I'll give her.   _____

We are sitting.   _____

They brought it.   _____

I'll tell her.   _____

Don't hit it.   _____

We won't buy it.   _____

I should read.   _____

Read!   _____

I heard you.   _____

5.   Identify the verb modifiers in the following.

/khub astom/ "I'm fine."	**Adjective**
/raftan khaana/ "They went home."	_____
/aastaa narow/ "Don't go slowly."	_____
/delem meysha ke akhbaara gowsh konom/ "I want to listen to the news."	_____
/ketaab-e pashtowra gereftom/ "I read the Pashto book."	_____
/gapeta tekraar kow/ "Repeat what you said."	_____
/emrowz myaayan/ "They are coming today."	_____
/englisi gap zada meytaani? / "Can you speak English?"	_____
/amrikaara didi?/ "Have you been to America?"	_____

3

The Noun Phrase

Nouns, like verbs, fall into a distinct category. They denote names, persons, animals, objects, happenings and events, take inflections and derivations, and have specific functions, and modifiers (dependents). Nouns are divided into mass/count, concrete/abstract, proper/common and others.

Noun Inflections

Noun formation involves inflections and derivations. Inflectionally, they take the plural, object and possessive markers. Derivations make it possible to derive nouns from verbs and adjectives, and to change one type of noun into another. We discuss noun inflections first and deal with the derivatives later in the chapter.

The plural. As the following examples illustrate, the plural suffix is {-aa} attached to a noun. Note that if the noun ends with /i/, it changes to /y/ (#5), and if the last vowel is /u/ it becomes /w/ (#4) before the plural marker. Finally, if the noun ends in /a/, it drops before the plural marker (#1 and #3).

Examples:

Singular	Plural
1. /khaana/ "house/room"	khaan**aa**/ "houses/rooms"
2. /maktab/ "school"	/maktab**aa**/ "schools"
3. /khalta/ "bag"	/khalt**aa**/ "bags"
4. /chaaqu/ "knife"	/chaaq**waa**/ "knives"

5. /chawki/ "chair"   /chawkyaa/ "chairs"

6. /molaa/ "cleric"   /molaaaa/ "clerics"

Use of the Plural Noun

Unlike English, a common noun without the plural marker can refer to one entity (singular) or more than one (plural). For example, /ma ketaab daarom/ could mean either "I have a book" or "I have books." Here, the emphasis is not on the number but on its existence. If the listener wants to know the number, he would ask: /chand ketaab daari/ "How many books do you have?" Thus to say "Do you have any books?" in Dari, the accurate question would be "/ketaab daari? /, not */ketaabaa dari? /. Violation of this rule leads to awkward and ungrammatical sentences. This happens frequently in the media, including VOA and BBC, when translating from English into Dari or vice versa. For example, translating "The library has books," into *4 /ketaabkhaana ketaabaa daara/ is ungrammatical or "Denglish." The accurate translation is /ketaabkhaana ketaab daara/.

When quantifiers or unit nouns modify a noun, it is always in the singular. Thus, /do ketaab/ but not */do ketaabaa/ "two books" or /do daana ketaab/ "two (copies of) books."

The Object Marker

Another noun inflection in Dari is the object marker. The presence of the object marker indicates definiteness unless the verb is /khosh daashtan/ "to like," whose object always takes the object marker, regardless of whether it is definite or indefinite. Hence, /ketaab meykhaayom/ means "I want one or more than one book," whereas /ketaaba meykhayom/ means "I want **the** book." Almost all Dari verbs are of the latter type. Verbs that always require the object marker are rare. Perhaps, /khosh daashtan/ "to like" is the only one in the language. As the following examples illustrate, the object marker {-a} has two variations or allomorphs: {-a} after a consonant (#1 and #5) and {-ra} after a vowel(#2, #3, #4, and #6). Finally, all proper nouns (#3 and #5) and pronouns (#6) must have the object marker regardless of the nature of the verb perhaps because they are definite.

---

4   A star (*) means the construction under discussion is ungrammatical.

Examples:

1. /ketaab**a** kharidom/ "I bought **the** book."
2. /chawki**ra** gereftom/ "I took/got **the** chair."
3. /alima**ra** didom/ "I saw Halima."
4. /ketaabaa**ra** aawordom/ "I brought **the** books."
5. /entezaa**ra** goftom/ "I told Entezar."
6. /unaa**ra** goftom/ "I told them."

Pronouns

Pronouns are a subclass of nouns that include pointer words (demonstrative pronouns), possessives, personal and reflexive pronouns. They are a subclass of nouns because they function as noun head or nucleus of a noun phrase, as in /ma aamadom/ "I came," where the pronoun /ma/ "I" fills the noun phrase slot as the subject of the sentence. Pronouns are either free or bound.

Free Pronouns

Free pronouns are illustrated in the following table:

	Singular	**Plural**
First Person	/ma/ "I"	/maa/ "we"
Second Person	/tu/ "you" singular or familiar	/shomaa/ "you" plural or formal/polite
Third Person	/u/ "he/she"	/unaa/ "they"

Genitive Pronouns

Apart from the plural and the object marker, Dari nouns and pronouns are inflicted with genitive (possessive pronoun) and addition. Thus:

	Singular	**Plural**
First Person:	/ketaabe**m**/ "**my** book"	/ketaabe**maa**/ "**our** book"
Second Person:	/ketaaabe**t**/ "**your** book"	/ketabe**taan**/ "**your** book"
Third Person:	/ketaabe**sh**/ "**his/her** book"	/ketaabesh**aan**/ "**their** book"

	Singular	Plural
First Person	**-m**	**-maa**
Second Person	**-t**	**-taan**
Third Person	**-sh**	**-shaan**

Examples:

	Singular	Plural
First Person	ketaabe**m**	Ketaabe**maa**
Second Person	ketaabe**t**	Ketaabe**taan**
Third Person	ketaabe**sh**	Ketaabe**shaan**

It is important to note that the suffix {-e} preceding the genitive marker is the Izafa, connecting the word modified to the modifier. That is why the word /ketaabem/ "my book" consists of three morphemes: /ketaab/, {-e} and {-m}, where the word modified, /ketaab/, is connected to the modifier, the genitive with the Izafa. This will be made clearer if we consider the underlying or deep structure of the construction. The construction /ketaabem/ "my book," is derived from /ketaab-e ma/ "my book," where the genitive {-m} replaces /ma/. Thus the long form(emphatic) is the underlying structure of the short version or contracted form, /ketaabem/.

Examples:

Emphatic	Non-Emphatic
/ketaab-e **ma**/ "**my** book"	/ketaabe**m**/ "my book"
/ketaab-e **maa**/ "**our** book"	/ketaabe**maa**/ "our book"
/ketaab-e **u**/ "**his/her** book"	/ketaabe**shaan**/ "their book"
/ketaab-e **tu**/ "**your** (sing) boom"	/ketaabe**t**/ "Your book"
/ketaab-e **shomaa**/ "**your** (pl) book" /	/ketaabe**taan**/ "your book"

Note that the genitive for the third person plural is made from the third person singular by adding {-aan}: /ketaabe**sh**/ and / ketaabe**shaan**/.

It is worth mentioning here that the use of Dari genitive for the third person is different from English. For example, out of context, the English sentence "Karim read his book," could mean either "He/She read his/her own book or someone else's." But in Dari, this construction has a different meaning. The construction /karim ketaabesha khaand/ only means "Karim read someone else's book", not his own. To say "Karim read his own book," the word {khod} "self" must be added to express such a meaning: /karim ketaab-e khoda khaand/. This is a mistake frequently made when translating from English. An English sentence such as "Hamid Karzai arrested his brother," cannot be translated into Dari as /karzay beraadar-esha destgir kad/. Instead, it should be: /karzay beraadar-e khoda destgir kad. /This mistake in translation occurs in Afghan radio and television broadcasts, including those from the BBC and VOA.

Addition

To express addition, {-aam} is suffixed to proper and common nouns as well as prounouns:

1. /karim**aam** mariz-as/ "Karim is sick, **too.**" Yes!
2. /ketaab**aam** qimat-as/ "Books are expensive, **too.**"
3. /m**aam** malem-astom/ "I'm a teacher, **too.**"
4. /tuw**aam** mariz-asti/. "You are sick, **too.**"
5. /w**aam** mariz-as/ "He/She is sick, **too.**"
6. /shom**aam** mariz-asteyn/ "You (plural) are sick, **too.**"
7. /un**aam** mariz-astan/ "They are sick, **too.**"
8. /m**aam** mariz-asteym/ "We are sick, **too.**"
9. /chaaqw**aam** teyz-as/ "The knife is sharp, **too.**"
10. ghazny**aam** garm neys/ "Ghazni is not warm, **either.**"

Please note that, if a word ends with the vowel /a/ (#3) or /aa/ (#6 and#8), it drops before {-aam}. Thus, /ma/+ {-aam} and /shomaa/+ {-aam}/ respectively become /maam/ and /shomaam/. Simliarly, if the noun or pronoun ends with /u/ or /i/, these vowels become /w/ or /y/ respectively. Hence, /tu/+ {-aam} becomes /twaam/ (#4), while /ghazni/+ {-aam} turns into /ghaznyaam/ (#10). The same is the case with #9, where the vowel /u/ in /chaaqu/ "knife" becomes /w/. Furthermore, all proper nouns (#1 and #10) and common nouns (#2 and #9), as well as all pronouns (#3, #4, #5, #6, #7 and #8) can be suffixed this way to express addition or inclusion. Finally, the suffix {-aam} is used in both affirmative and negative sentences without any additional changes in the sentence. This is different from English where "too" is used in the former and "either" in the latter. Compare "He is a teacher, too" and "He is not a teacher, either."

Reflexive Pronouns

The genitive marker is suffixed to the word {khod] "self" to generate reflexive pronouns. Thus:

First person: /khode**m**/ "myself" /khode**ma**/ "ourselves"
Second person: /khode**t**/ "yourself" /khode**taan**/ "yourselves"
Third person: /khode**sh**/ "himself" /khode**shaan**/ "themselves"

	Singular	Plural
First person	khodem	khodemaa
Second person	khodet	khodetaan
Third person	khodesh	khodeshaan

Interrogative Pronouns

The interrogative pronouns are /ki/ "who" /kojaa/ "where" /chi/ "what" /kay/ "when" /chand/ "how much" and so on. They can be called k-ch pronouns because they all begin with /k/ or /ch/.

Examples:

/**ki** aamad/ "**Who** came?"
/**chi** mekhaayi/ "**What** do you want?"
/**kojaa** miri/ "**Where** are you going?"
/**kay** az amrikaa aamad/ "**When** did he come from America?"
/**chand** meykhaayi/ "**How much** do you want?"

These words are pronouns because they function as nouns as the following examples illustrate.

Noun	Pronoun
/**karim** raft/ "Karim left."	/**ki** raft/ "**Who** left?"
/**reshwat** da afghaanestaan zyaad-as/	/**chi** da afghaanestaan zyaad-as/ "**What** is rampant in Afghanistan?"
/**dirowz** aamad/ "He came yesterday."	/**kay** aamad/ "**When** did he come?"
/ketaab **bist daalar**-as/ "The is $20."	/ketaab **chand**-as/ "**How much** is the book?"

Point Pronouns

Pointer words fall into a specific category of pronouns. Use of the word "pointer" is perhaps more descriptive than the word "demonstrative," because they point to objects near or away from the speaker; {i} "this" and {yaa} "these" belong to the former while {u} "that," and {waa} "those" to the latter. These pointer nouns do not just differ in meaning, but they also differ in how they function in a sentence. For example, {i} and {u} function as noun modifiers, but not {yaa} and {waa}. Thus /i ketaab/ "this book" and /u ketaab" "that book" but not */yaa ketaabaa/ "these books/ or*/waa ketaabaa/ "those books." When the modified noun is singular, /i/ "this" and /u/ "that" respectively mean "this"(#1) and "that." (#3) However, when the noun is in the plural, /i/ means "these" (#2) and /u/ "those,"(#4) as in the following examples. This difference may be problematic for native speakers learning Dari.

Examples:

1. /i ketaab/ "this book"
2. /i ketaabaa/ "these books"
3. / u ketaab/ "this book"
4. /u ketaabaa/ "those books

Personal Pronouns

As it has been pointed, Dari has both free and bound pronouns. The genitives, discussed earlier, are bound pronouns as they are attached to the noun. Personal pronouns are free when they occur in isolation without being attached, as in the following table.

	Singular	Plural
First Person	ma "I"	maa "we"
Second Person	tu "You" sing/familiar	shomaa "you" pl./formal
Third Person	u "he/she/it"	waa /unaa "they"

Just as there is no gender, Dari grammar does not make a distinction between the nominative "he/ she/" and the accusative "him/her" either. Compare /u malem-as/ "He/She is a teacher," and /karim ura did/ "Karim saw him/her."
Pronouns of indefinite reference: / kas-e/ "one-who": /aadam/ "one" and /**meygan**/ "they say or it is said." An indefinite pronoun does not have a specific reference; it is generic.

Examples:

1. /**kas-e** ke tambal-as peyshraft nameykona/ "**One** who is lazy does not advance."

2. /**aadam** ke da amrika meyra ayraan meymaana/ "When one goes to America, one finds it surprising."

3. /**kas** ke meymaan meysha baayad naawakht nayaaya/ "When **one** is invited, He/she should not arrive late."

4. /**megan** ke dorowgh faayda nadaara/ "They say that lying is not useful."

Note that the indefinite pronoun {kas} is used with or without the Izafa, as in (#1) and (#3) and the pronoun{-an} "they" is suffixed only with the present stem of /goftan/ "telling/saying."

Common and Proper Nouns

Like English, Dari makes a distinction between common and proper nouns. Semantically, common nouns denote generalities, while proper nouns refer to specific names of people and places. Syntactically, proper nouns are usually not pluralized whereas common nouns are. Thus /ketaabaa/ "books" but not */entezaaraa/ "the Entezars." In English orthography, proper nouns are also capitalized but not in Dari because capitalization does not exist in its writing system.

Count and Mass Concrete Nouns

Nouns are also divided into mass and count. Count nouns are used to refer to objects (things, animals, people, and so on) that can be counted (*book, bird, and teacher*). Unlike mass nouns, count nouns have singular and plural forms (*books, birds, and teachers*). Mass nouns, on the other hand, involve liquid and solid objects and concepts, and they do not take the plural marker: water, iron, love. Count nouns and mass nouns also differ in other respects. Count and mass nouns, usually have different predeterminers. For example, the quantifier /chand/ "how many" is usually used with count nouns and /cheqa/ "how much" with mass nouns. Thus /chand ketaab/ means "how many books" but /cheqa bura/ means "how much sugar."

Abstract Nouns

Abstraction refers to events, states, feelings, ideas, and other abstracts. Unlike count and mass nouns, they are not concrete in that they cannot be touched, felt or seen. Consider, for example, abstract nouns such as /ghayrat/ "courage" and /sedaaqat/ "honesty."

Abstract nouns can be mass or count in the sense of whether they can be pluralized. This differs from language to language. Unlike English, Dari /khoshi/

"happiness," for example, is a count noun because one can say /khoshyaa/, but not */ghayrataa/ "courages." One cannot say, however, *"happinesses" in English. More examples are provided below.

Count Abstract Nouns	Mass Abstract Nouns
/khoshi/ "happiness"	/ghayrat/ "courage"
/jang/ "war/fight"	/imaan/ "faith, belief"
/kheyaanat/ "treason"	/sedaaqat/ "honesty"
/tajroba/ "experience/experiment"	/ezat/ "honor"

Unit Nouns

To divide mass and count nouns into parts, unit nouns or classifiers are used. Unlike written Dari, spoken Dari makes use of a relatively smaller number of unit nouns. For example, /yak **raas** asp/ means "one horse" in written Dari but /yak **daana** asp/ in spoken. Some frequently used unit nouns in spoken Dari include /daana/ "piece," /darjan/ "dozen," /jwaal/ "sack," and /jowra/ "pair" and /geylaas/ "glass".In the following examples, unit nouns are highlighted.

/yak **jowra** boot/ "a pair of shoes"	Mass
/yak **darjan** tokhm/ "A dozen of eggs"	Count
/yak **jowra** gowshwaara/ "a pair of earrings"	Count
/yak **beshqaab** palaw/ "a plate of rice"	Mass
/yak **daana** qalam/ "one pen"	Count
/yak gelaas aw/ / "one glass of water"	Mass
/yak **khalta** bura/ "a bag of sugar"	Mass
/yak **daana** asp/ "One horse"	Count
/yak **jwaal** aard/ "one sack of flour"	Mass
/do **darjan** pyaala/ "two dozens of cups"	Count
/yak **bowtal** shir/ "a bottle of milk"	Mass
/yak **seyr** aard/ "**one seer** (14 pounds) of flour"	Mass
/yak [5]**kharwaar** chowb/ "one kharwaar (1120 pounds) of firewood"	Count

---

[5]   A /seyr/ is about 14 pounds and 80 seyrs make a /kharwaar/.

Group Nouns

Group nouns refer to a set of objects that can be singular or plural. Some group nouns include /lashkar/ "army," /gorow/ "group," /gala/ "herd," /rama/ "herd," /qataar/ "flock," /daara/ "gang," /sepaa/ "army," /qabila/ "tribe," /tim/ "team," /anjoman/ "association," and /qawm/ "a community with common interests," as in the following examples:

1. /**lashkar**-e eslaam/ "the army of Islam," /sepaa saalaar/ "commander-in-chief/chief of the army"
2. /**daar-e** doz/ "a **gang** of thieves," /**qataar**-e shotor/ "a **flock** of camels,"
3. /**gal**-ey morghaa/ "a **flock** of chickens," /**qawm**-e taajek/ "the Tajik **ethnic goup**," /**tim**-e fowtbaal/ "a football **team**," /**anjoman**-e zanaan-e afghaanestaan/ "The Women's **Association** of Afghanistan"
4. /**ram**-ey boz/ "a **herd** of goats"

It should be pointed in this connection that, in such contructions, the Izafa follows the group nouns. However, when a quantifier is employed, the Izafa is optional. For example, /yak gala gowsfand/ and /yak gal-ey gowsfand/ "one flock of sheep." Are both grammatical.

Part Nouns

Part nouns refer to parts of objects or their whole. Some part nouns in Dari are: /nesf/ or /nim/ "half," /kol/ or /tamaam/ "whole," /towta/ "piece," /parcha/ "part/piece," /chaarak/ "a quarter," and /gowsha/ "corner/ slice."

Examples:

/**nesf-e** keyk/ "**half of** the cake" /**kol-e** naan/ "**the whole** bread"
/**chaarak-e** ma.ash/ "**one-fourth** of the salary" /yak **towta** zamin/ "**a piece of** land"
/yak **paarcha** teka/ "**a piece of** cloth" /**tamaam-e** mardom/ "**all of** the people"
/yak **gowsh-e** khaana/ "**a corner of** the room" /yak **zara** gowsht/ "**a little bit of** meat"

Note that, like group nouns, in such phrases, the Izafa is optional when a quantifier is present. Compare /yak towta zamin/ "one piece of land" and /towt-ey zamin/ "a piece of land." The only exception to this rule is perhaps part nouns such as /nesf/ "half" whick always takes the Izafa with or without a quantifier. Compare /nesf-e naan/ and /yak nesf-e naan/.

Derivative Nouns

Apart from inflections such as the plural, the genitive and the object markers, nouns are also marked with derivatives. It is important to remember from the previous chapter that inflections are regular, while derivatives are irregular and can change the grammatical class of the word they are attached to. Nouns can be derived from verbs and adjectives. Some common noun markers are:{-i}, {-esh}, and {-an}. Other noun markers change a simple noun to a complex one.

1) From Adjectives

a) By adding {-i}

The suffix changing adjectives to nouns is {-i}, which has three allomorphs (variants): [-i], {-gi} and {-yi}. The suffix is {-i} if the adjective ends with a consonant, {-gi} after /a/, and {-yi} after /aa/, as in the following examples.

Adjective	Noun
/sard/ "cold"	/sardi/ "coldness"
/garm/ "hot"	/garmi/ "heat"
/nazdik/ "close"	/nazdiki/ "closeness"
/syss/ "black"	/syaayi/ "blackness"
/daraaz/ "long"	/daraazi/ "length"
/kata/ "big/ huge"	/katagi/ "bigness"
/chaalaak/ "shrewd"	/chaalaaki/ "shrewdness"
/khub/ "good"	/khubi/ "goodness"
/bad/ "bad"	/badi/ "evil"
/aaraam/ "quiet/ peaceful"	/aaraami/ "peace"
/qimat/ "expensive/pricy"	/qimati/ "price"
/jowaan/ "young"	/jowaaani/ "youth"
/kowtaa/ "short"	/kowtaayi/ "shortness"
/safaa/ "clean"	/safaayi/ "cleanliness"
/sharmenda/ "shameful"	/sharmendagi/ "shamefulness"
/maanda/ "tired"	/maandagi/ "tiredness"

b) **By adding {-esh}**

The constructions /khubesh/ and /khubaaysh/ mean "the good one" and "the good ones". The construction /khubesh/ consists of three morphemes: {khub},{-e} and {-sh}. The addition of the plural to the second construction makes it a combination of four morphemes. When {-esh} is added to an adjective, the result is a definite noun because such constructions always take the object marker {-a} or {-ra} in the presence of a transitive verb. Thus /khubesha kharidom/ means "I bought the good one," and /khubaaysha kharidom/ means "I bought the good ones."

Examples

Adjective	Singular Noun	Plural Noun
/khub/ "good"	/khubesh/ "the good one"	/khubaaysh/ "the good ones"
/kharaab/ "bad"	/kharaabesh/ "the bad one"	/kharaabaayesh/ "the bad ones"
/paak/ "clean"	/paakesh/ "the clean one"	/paakaayesh/ "the clean ones"
/kalaan/ "big"	/kalaanesh/ "the big one"	/kalaanaayesh/ "the big ones"
/khord/ "small"	/khordesh/ "the small one"	/khordaayesh/ "the small ones"
/arzaan/ "cheap"	/arzaanesh/ "the cheap one"	/arzaanaaysh/ "the cheap ones"
/daraaz/ "long/tall"	/daraazesh/ "the long one"	/daraazaash/ "the long ones"

2) From Verbs

a) **By adding {-esh} to present stems**

Verb	Noun
/-khor-/ "eat"	/khoresh/ "feed"
/-saaz-/ "make"	/saazesh/ "cutting a deal"
/-maal-/ "rub"	/maalesh/ "for rubbing"
/-gard-/ "walk"	/gardesh/ "a walk"
/-daw-/ "run"	/dawesh/ "running"
/-khaar-/ "scratch/itch"	/khaaresh/ "itching"

Noun

a) By adding {-an} to the past stems

Verb	Noun (Gerund)
/-raft-/ "went"	/raftan/ "going"
/-goft-/ "told"	/goftan/ "saying/talking"
/-aamad-/ "came"	/aamadan/ "coming"
/-bud-/ "was"	/bodan/ or /budan/ "being"
/-khaand/ "read"	/khaandan/ "reading"
/kad/ "did"	/kadan/ "doing"
/did/ "saw"	/didan/ "seeing"
/kharid/ "bought"	/kharidan/ "buying"

3) From Nouns

Common nouns are changed to agentive nouns (nouns that refer to someone who performs an action related to the meaning of the noun) by the addition of the following suffixes: {-**gar**} "doing," /-saa**z**} "making," {-**zan**} "hitting," {-**baaz**} "playing," {-gowy} "telling/saying," {-**daar**-} "having," {-**waan**} "owning/running/ keeping," and {-**daan**-} "knowing," as in the following examples.

Common Noun	Agentive Noun
/zar/ "gold"	/zargar/ "a goldsmith"
/aayin/ "iron"	/aayengar/ "a blacksmith"
/qesa/ "story"	/qesagowy/ "a story teller"
/dorowgh/ "a lie"	/dorowghgowy/ "a liar"
/chawki/ "chair"	/chawkisaaz/ "a chair maker"
/alabi/ "tin"	/alabisaaz/ "a tinsmith"
/chana/ "bargain"	/chanazan/ "a bargainer"
/khesht/ "brick"	/kheshtzan/ "a brick layer"
/laaf/ "boast"	/laafzan/ "one who boasts"
/kaftar/ "pigeon"	/kaftarbaaz/ "pigeon flier"
/sag/ "dog"	/sagbaaz/ "a dog owner" whose dog participates in dog fights"
/bacha/ "boy"	/bachabaz "a homosexual"
/zanaka/ "woman"	/zanakabaaz/ "a womanizer"
/zobaan/ "tongue/language"	/zobaandaan/ "a polyglot"
/taarikh/ "history"	/taarikhdaan/ "a historian"

—

61

/dowkaan/ "shop"	/dowkaandaar/ "a shopkeeper"
/paysa/ "money"	/paysadaar/ "rich, wealthy"
/kaar/ "work"	/kaargar/ "a worker"
/mowtar/ "car"	/mowtarwaan/ "a driver"
/gaadi/ "cart, buggy"	/gaadiwaan/ "a buggy/cart driver

Simple, Complex and Compound Nouns

A noun in Dari can be simple, complex, or compound in its form. A complex noun has a suffix. More accurately, a complex noun is a combination of a free morpheme and one or more than one bound morphemes. Thus, / maktab/ "school" is simple while /makatbaa/ "schools" is complex. In compound nouns, however, two free morphemes are combined. For example, /dawaakhaana/ "drugstore/pharmacy" is a combination of /dawaa/ "medicine" and "khaana/ "room/ house/place."

Compound nouns should not be confused with noun phrases. Dari compound nouns do not have the Izafa. Thus, /kow-ye safeyd/ "a white mountain" is a noun phrase because the word /kow/ "mountain" is connected to its modifier, /safeyd/ "white," with the Izafa. Therefore, /kow-ye safeyd/ is a noun phrase, not a compound. On the other hand, /safeydkow/ "White Mountains" in eastern Afghanistan, is a compound noun because the Izafa is absent in the construction. In English, stress distinguishes a noun phrase such as "a white house" and a compound noun such as "the White House." In a noun phrase, the primary stress is on the second word, whereas in a compound it is not. The same is true in the case of "the black bird" and "a black bird." This phonological distinction, however, does not exist in Dari because the primary stress always falls on the last syllable of nouns.

Thus:

1. **Noun+/khaana/**

Simple Noun	Compound Noun
/dawaa/ "medicine/drug"	/dawaakhaana/ "drugstore"
/chaay/ "tea"	/chaaykhaana/ "tea house"
/maashin/ "machine"	/maashinkhaana/ "factory"
/aashpaz/ "cook"	/aashpazkhaana/ "kitchen"
/shafaa/ "cure"	/shafaakhaana/ "hospital"

/meymaan/ "guest"	/meymaankhaana/ "guesthouse"
/kaa/ "hay"/	/kaakhaana/ "barn"
/qemaar/ "gambles"	/qemaarkhaana/ "gambling house"
/paaru/ "manure"	/paarukhaana/ "manure storage"
/sharaab/ "wine/liquor"	/sharaabkhaana/ "a bar"

2. **Noun+/baagh/** (garden/orchard)

Simple Noun	Compound Noun
/angur/ "grape"	/angurbaagh/ "grape orchard"
/taak/ "vine"	/taakbaagh/ "vineyard"
/anaar/ "pomegranate"	/anaarbaagh/ "pomegranate orchard"
/meywa/ "fruit"	/meywabaagh/ "orchard"

3. {**sar-**} "head/ chief" +**Noun**

Simple Noun	Compound Noun
/malem/ "teacher"	/sarmalem/ "head teacher"
/kaateb/ "clerk"	/sarkaateb/ "head clerk"
/kheyl/ "group/tribe"	/sarkheyl/ "(tribal) leader"
/edaara/ "administration"	/saredaara/ "director"
/monshi/ "secretary"	/sarmonshi/ "General Secretary"
/maqaala/ "article"	/sarmaqaala/ "editorial"

4. **By adding an adjective to a noun**

Adjective+ noun	Proper Compound Noun
/safeyd/ "white"+ /kow/ "mountain"	/safeydkow/ "white mountain"
/syaa/ "black" +/kow/	/syaakow/ "black mountain"
/syaa/ +/baagh/ "garden"	/syaabaagh/ "black jungle"
/syaa/ + /daana/ "grain"	/syaadaana/ "a kind of herb"
/syaa/ +/sang/ "stone"	/syaasang/ "a place near Kabul" ("black stone")

5. By adding a cardinal number to a noun

Number+Noun	Compound Noun
/chaar/ "four" +/su/ "side"	/chaarsu/ "a cross section"
/chaaar/+ /baagh/ "garden"	/chaarbaagh/ "perhaps a square or rectangular orchard"
/chaar/ + /raa/ "road"	/charraayi/ "cross section/crossroads"
/now/ "nine" +/borj/ "tower"	/nowborja/ "a fort with nine towers"
/chaar/ "four"+/konj/ "corner"	/chaarkonja/ "rectangular"
/aft/ "seven" +/meywa/ "fruit"	/aftmeywa/ "mixture of seven dried fruits"
/chaar/ +/masaala/ "spice"	/chaarmasaala/ "a special spice consisting of four different spices"
/chaar/ +/maghz/ "nut"	/chaarmaghz/ "walnut"

Noun Structure and Functions

A noun phrase has head and modifiers. In a noun phrase, the head is obligatory while the modifiers are optional. Nouns also have functions: subject, object, predicate, object of a prepositional phrase, as in the following examples:

Noun Functions

1. /**ketaab**/ arzaan as/ "The book is cheap." **Noun (Subject)**
2. /karim **khaana** kharid/ "Karim bought a house." **Noun (Object)**
3. /**ketaab-e englisi** qimat-as/ "An English book is expensive." **NP (Subject)**
4. /jowaab **da ketaab**—as / "The answer is in the book." **Prepositional Phrase(Adverb).**
5. /ketaab-e [**dari**] arzaan-as/ "The Dari book is cheap." **Noun Phrase (Modifier)**
6. /i **ketaab**-as/ "This is a book." **Noun (Predicate)**

Noun Modifiers

Some modifiers occur before (pre-modifiers) and others after nouns (post-modifiers). We deal with the former first and discuss the latter next.

Pre-Modifiers

Pre-modifiers are adjectives (Adj), point pronouns (PPro), cardinal numbers (CN), part nouns (PN), unit nouns (UN) and quantifiers (Q).

Examples:

1. /**ketaab**/ "a/the book" **Head**
2. /**i** ketaab/ "this book" **PPro**
3. /**do** ketaab/ "two books" **CN**
4. /**besyaar** ketaab/ "many books" **Q**
5. /**yak darjan** ketaab/ "one dozen of books" **CN+UN**
6. /**baaz-e** ketaabaa/ "some books" **PN**
7. /**chand daana** ketaab/ "a few numbers of books" **Q+UN**
8. /**i daa daana** ketaab/ "these ten copies books" **PPro+CN +UN**
9. /**baaz-e i daa daana** ketaab/ "some of these ten books" **PN+PPro+CN+UN**
10. /**baaz-e i chaar darjan** ketaab/ **"some of these four dozen books" PN+PPr+CN+UN**
11. /**yak khub** ketaab/ "a good book" **CN+Adjective** (Emphatic)
12. /**yak besyaar khub** ketaab/ "a very good book" **CN+Q+Adj**
13. /**i khub** ketaab/ "this good book" **PPro+Adj**
14. /**i do khub** ketaab/ "these two good books" **PPro+CN+Adj**
15. /**arzaantarin** ketaab/ "the cheapest book" **Adj-super/Super Ordinal Number**
16. /awalin ketaab/ "the very first book" **Ordinal-Superlative**

Note that a) with a part noun (6), the head noun is always in the plural and with a cardinal number and quantifier it is in the singular (3,7,8,9); b) an adjective may premodify a noun for emphasis (11,12, and 13); c) The maximum number of premodifiers in the absence of an adjective cannot exceed four (10) and the order of modifiers is fixed **PN+PPro+CN+UN;** d) In the presence of a simple adjective, the number of modifiers does not exceed three (12) and the order of modifiers is also fixed (14): **CN+Q-Adj** (12) or **PPro+CN+Adj** (14); f) and, finally, when the modifier is a superlative adjective or superlative ordinal number, usually no other modifiers are allowed (15 and 16).

The discussion on the types and order of premodifiers can be summed up as follows:

Rule # 1. **Q+Head**
Rule # 2. **PN+PPro+CN+UN +Head**

Rule # 3. **CN+Q+Adj +Head**
Rule # 4. **PPro+CN+Adj+Head**
Rule # 5. **Adj-super +Head**

Rule #1 states that when a quantifier is the pre-modifier, no other modifiers are permitted. Thus, /besyaar ketaab/ but not /*yak besyaar ketaab/ or* /baaz-e besyaar ketaab/ or any other modifiers except the quantifier.

Rule #2 indicates that when point nouns, part nouns, cardinal numbers, and unit nouns premodify a noun, they have to be in a certain order. Violation of this rule can lead to ungrammatical constructions. For example, cardinal numbers must precede unit nouns, point pronouns must come before, the two, and part nouns must precede all the other modifiers as in /baaz-e u daa daana ketaab/ but not any other sequence. Thus, */da daana u ketaab/ or */ daana u daa ketaab/, */ da daana u baaz-e ketaab/and other combinations are ungrammatical.

Rule #3 means that when an adjective is one of the pre-modifiers, the other pre-modifiers allowed are cardinal numbers and quantity words. Furthermore, the cardinal number usually precedes the quantity word, and the adjective must follow both. Thus, / yak besyaar khub ketaab/ but not */khub besyaar yak ketaab/ or */yak khub besyaar ketaab/. And finally, in such constructions, the adjective is in its simple form, i.e., without any suffix.

Rule #4, on the other hand, means that in the presence of an adjective, point pronouns and cardinal numbers can also occur as pre-modifiers. However, the point pronoun must come before the cardinal number, and they both precede the adjective. Thus, /u sey khub ketaab/ but not */khub u sey ketaab/, */u khub sey ketaab/ or */sey u khub ketaab/. Here too, the adjective is in its simple form.

Finally, rule #5 states that in the presence of a comparative or superlative adjective, no other premodifiers are allowed. Thus, /khubtar ketaab/ or / khubtarin ketaab/ but not * / u khubtar ketaab/, */baaz-e khubtar ketaab/, */do khubter ketaab/ or any other construction containing modifiers other than the comparative or superlative adjectives. It is important to note that with superlative adjectives as premodifiers, the noun can be singular or plural. However, there is one adjective, /besyaari/ "most," that requires the noun to be in the plural. Hence, /khubtarin ketaab/ or /beytarin ketaaba/ but only /besyaari ketaabaa/ "most books," not /besyaari ketaab/.

Emphasis and Contrast

Emphasis or contrast is expressed in a variety of ways. Pre-modification is one mechanism; using a separate subject, intonation, and cleft transformation also serve the same purpose.

Examples:

Nonemphatic	Emphatic
/ketaab-e khub/ "a good book"	/khub ketaab/ "a good book" (Pre-modifier)
/nafar-e awal/ "the first person"	/awal nafar/ "the first person" (Pre-modifier)
/raftom/ "I went."	/ma raftom/ "I went." (Separate subject)
/didomesh/ "I saw him/her/it."	/karima didom/ "I saw Karim." (Separate object)
/ma meyrom/ "I'm going."	/ma meyrom "I am going." (Intonation: Primary stress (')
/karim khaanara kharid/ "Karim bought the house."	/i karim bud ke khaanara kharid/ "It was Karim who bought the house.

(Cleft)

Post-modifiers

Noun post-modifiers include adjectives, genitives, pronouns, nouns, prepositional phrases (PP), and clauses.

Examples:

1. /ketaab-e **ma**/ "**my** book"	**Genitive Pronoun** (Free)
2. /ketaab-e **karim**/ "Karim's book"	**Genitive Noun**
3. /ketaab-e **Dari**/ "A/the Dari book"	**Noun**
4. /ketaab-e **qimat**/ "Expensive book/s"	**Adjective** (Non-emphatic)
5. /ketaab-e **sar-e meyz**/ "the book on the table"	**PP** (Predicate)
6. /ketaab-e **ke ma mekhaayom**/ "The book that I want"	**Clause**
7. /ketaab, **rafiq-e ensaan**/ "Books, man's friend."	**Opposition**
8. /karim, **beraadar-e ma**/ "Karim, my brother"	**Opposition**
9. /molaa omar **yaa raabar-e taalebaan**/ "Mullah Omar or Taliban's leader"	**Opposition**

Unlike pre-modifiers, most post-modifiers are connected to the head with the Izafa, the exception being the appositive construction (7, 8, and 9). In an appositive construction, the modifier and the word modified refer to the same person or object. For example, /karim/ and /najaar/ in (9) refer to the same person. Additionally, in a chain of post-modifiers, the last word does not have the Izafa because no words follow to be also connected. Thus, /ketaab-**e** kalaan-**e** englisi-**ye** karim/means "Karim's big English book." Finally, almost all post-modifiers of nouns are reduced to relative clauses. For example, /ketaab-e ma/ is the reduced form of /ketaab az ma-s/ "The book is mine." Similarly, / ketaab-e qimat/ is derived from /ketaab qimat-as/ "The book is expensive." Relative and other clauses are discussed in chapter 6.

Awal and Awalin

Unlike English, Dari ordinal numbers take the superlative {-in}. Take / awal/ and /awalin/, for example. These two words are both ordinal numbers except that the latter has the superlative adjective marker {-in} as in / qimattatrin/ "most expensive." Semantically, the word /awal/ means "first" and /awalin/ "a first" or "the very first." Syntactically, the ordinal number / awal/ can either premodify or post-modify a noun, depending on whether it is emphatic or not. Hence /nafar-e awal/ or /awal nafar/ means "the first person." The ordinal number /awalin/, on the other hand, can only be used as a premodifier: /awalin nafar/ but not /nafar-e awalin/. Finally, the use of the ordinal /awal/ "first," /dowom/ "second," and /seywom/ "third," and so on implies the existence of a series. For example, /nafar-e awal/ means there is more than one person standing in line to be mentioned in a sequence. But the use of /awalin/, /dowomin/, /sewomin/, and other "superlative" ordinals does not call for a series. Thus, "The first car in the world" can only be translated as /awalin mowtar-e donyaa/, not as /awal mowtar-e donyaa/. Here there is no question of the existence of other cars to be mentioned in a sequence because there had been none before. The Voice of America (VOA), talking about the first year of President Barak Obama in office on its Dari program in January 2010 said, /**awalin saal-e** reyaasat-e jamuri / instead of /**saal-e awal.**// The former is ungrammatical in Dari. Some more uses of the superlative ordinals are provided below.

Examples:

/awalin safir-e amrikaa da afghaanestan ki bud/ "Who was the first U.S ambassador in Afghanistan?"
/chaaromin jashn-e esteqlaal da kodaam saal bud/ "Which year was the fourth Independence celebration held?"
/awalin kas-e ke barqa ekhteraa kad ki bud/ "Who was the first person who invented electricity?"

/dowomin khaan-ey ke da kabol barq daasht kodaam bud/ "Which was the second house in Kabul which had electricity?"

/awalin orupaayi ke da afghaanestaan safar kad ke bud/ "Who was the first European who traveled to Afghanistan?"

Chapter Summary

Dari nouns take inflections and derivations. Noun inflections include the object marker, the genitive marker, and the plural marker. With derivatives, nouns are changed into adjectives, verbs, and other nouns. Nouns are simple, complex, or compound, and they are divided into concrete/abstract, common/proper, group nouns, pronouns, part nouns, and unit nouns, and so on.

Dari nouns have premodifiers and post-modifiers. The former include part and group nouns, quantifiers, cardinal numbers, and point pronouns. When a cardinal number modifies a noun, the head must be in the singular. The number of premodifiers cannot be more than four. When they do occur together, the order is: **PN+PPro+CN+UN+Head.** Most part nouns take the Izafa, and they require that the noun they modify always be in the plural. Post-modifiers are adjectives, free and bound genitive pronouns, nouns, prepositional phrases, and restrictive and nonrestrictive clauses. Emphasis is expressed by premodification, separate words, intonation, and cleft transformation. Finally, Dari nouns function as subject, predicate, object of the verb, and the preposition in clauses and sentences.

Exercises:

1. Are the following statements true (T) or false (F)?
F. The object marker attached to a noun always means the noun is definite.

_____ Inflections are irregular.

_____ Abstract nouns behave differently in different languages.

_____ Genitives in Dari can be either free or bound.

_____ Group nouns are inflicted in Dari.

_____ The presence of part nouns in a sentence requires that the noun it modifies must be in the plural form.

_____ The noun modified by a cardinal number is always in the singular.

_____ Adjectives usually precede the noun in a noun phrase.

_____ Post-modifiers are always connected to the noun with the Izafa.

_____ A noun without the plural marker could mean more than one.

_____ The object marker has two variations.

_____ Suffixed genitive pronouns in the third person is the same in English and Dari.

_____ Nouns can be used as premodifiers in Dari.

_____ Premodifiers in Dari cannot be more than five.

_____ Point pronouns in Dari are four.

_____ A compound noun has the Izafa.

_____ A noun is complex if it has an inflection.

_____ Dari Prouns are not suffixed.

2. Write formulas for the following noun phrases. The first is done for you.

/rafiq-e-khub-e entezaar/ "Entezar's good friend" **Head+Adj. +Genitive+Noun Head**

baaz-e mardom/ "some people

3. Write formulas for the following:

[See below for changes.]

/i ketaab-e dari/	Point Noun+ head+N
/baaz-e i qalamaa-ye amrikaayi/	_____
/ketaab-e englisi-ye beraadar-e karim/	_____
/chaay-e sowb/	_____
/i sey daana pyaala/	_____
/kol-e u chaar mowtar-e kalaan/	_____
/baaz-e i joraab-e amrikaayi/	_____
/baazaaraa-ye qadim-e kaabol/	_____
/i naan-e kalaan/	_____
/u dars-e englisi/	_____
/i ketaab-e dari/	_____
/baaz-e i qalamaa-ye amrikaayi/	_____
/ketaab-e englisi-ye beraadar-e karim/	_____
/chaay-e sowb/	_____
/kol-e u chaar mowtar-e kalaan/	_____
/baaz-e i joraab-e amrikaayi/	_____

/baazaaraa-ye kaabol/   _____

/i naan-e kalaan/   _____

/u dars-e faarsi/   _____

4.   Translate the following into English.

/daftar-e daaktar entezaar/   Dr. Entezar's office

/u chaa-ye sherin/   _____

/i chand jowra joraab/   _____

/naam-e beraadar-e karim/   _____

/u chaar jowra gowshwaara/   _____

/baaz-e i rowzaa-ye khub/   _____

/maari da daftar-as/   _____

/sefaarat-e amrikaa/   _____

/rowzaa-ye awal/   _____

/kampyutar-e beraadar-e entezaar/   _____

/shomaam faarsi meykhaaneyn/   _____

/tim-e fowtbaal-e kaabol/   _____

5.   Translate the following into Dari.

I'm from America.   /ma az amrikaa-stom/

Mary has four pairs of earrings.   _____

This is a Farsi book.   _____

All of these books are expensive.   _____

This tea is not that good.   _____

This house is very expensive.   _____

Take the good ones.   _____

Karim has two Dari books.   _____

This teacher is very capable.   _____

The post office is near the park.   _____

Karzai's brothers are also Afghanistanis.   _____

6. Write formulas for the following:
    [See below for changes.]

/i ketaab-e dari/	Point Noun+ head+N
/baaz-e i qalamaa-ye amrikaayi/	_____
/ketaab-e englisi-ye beraadar-e karim/	_____
/chaay-e sowb/	_____
/i sey daana pyaala/	_____
/kol-e u chaar mowtar-e kalaan/	_____
/baaz-e i joraab-e amrikaayi/	_____
/baazaaraa-ye qadim-e kaabol/	_____
/i naan-e kalaan/	_____
/u dars-e englisi/	_____
/i ketaab-e dari/	_____
/baaz-e i qalamaa-ye amrikaayi/	_____
/ketaab-e englisi-ye beraadar-e karim/	_____
/chaay-e sowb/	_____
/kol-e u chaar mowtar-e kalaan/	_____
/baaz-e i joraab-e amrikaayi/	_____
/baazaaraa-ye kaabol/	_____
/i naan-e kalaan/	_____
/u dars-e faarsi/	_____

4

The Adjectival Phrase

Introduction

Adjectives, too, fall into a class of their own. Like verbs, nouns and other word classes, they are defined on the basis of meaning, form and function. Semantically, an adjective denotes the quality of the thing named, indicates its quantity or extent, and specifies a thing as distinct from something else. Syntactically, adjectives modify nouns and verbs, and function as predicates. Finally, adjectives are divided into stative/gradable, attributive/predicative, simple/complex, compound, and so on.

Gradable and Stative Adjectives

Some adjectives are gradable while others are stative. Gradable adjectives express degree. That is why they have comparative and superlative forms. For example, /khub/ "good" is gradable because it can be suffixed with {-tar} as in /u ketaab khubtar-as/ "That book is better." Stative adjectives do not have comparative and superlative forms. Take /basta/ "closed" as an example. One cannot say */bastatar/. Still another difference between gradable and stative adjectives is that, the former can premodify nouns whereas the latter cannot. One can say, for example, /khub ketaab/ "a good book" but not * /basta ketaab/. Finally, gradable adjectives can be modified by adverbs of degree but stative adjectives cannot. Thus, it is grammatical to say /besyaar khub/ "very good," but not */besyaar basta/. Most adjectives in Dari are gradable.

Examples:

Graded Adjectives	Stative Adjectives
/khub/ "good"	/basta/ "closed"
/nezdik/ "close/near"	/mowrda/ "dead"
/dur/ "far"	/khalaas/ "finished"
/jowr/ "well"	/zenda/ "alive"
/mariz/ "sick"	/gom/ "lost"
/naajowr/ "sick"	/aazer/ "present"
/teyz/ "fast"	/ghayraazer/="absent"
/aasaan/ "easy"	/maalum/ "clear/known"

Comparatives and Superlatives

Comparing two objects is comparative; comparing one object with more than one refers to superlative. A comparative is formed by adding {-tar} to the basic adjective. The superlative, on the other hand, is made from the comparative by adding the suffix {-in} Thus:

Basic Adjective	Comparative	Superlative
/khub/ "good"	/khubtar/ "better"	/khubtarin/ "best"
/kharaab/ "bad"	/kharaabtar/ 'worse'	/kharaabtarin/ "worst"
/charb/ "greasy"	/charbtar/ "greasier"	/charbtarin/ "greasiest"
/bad/ "bad"	/badtar/ "worse"	/badtarin/ "worst"
/kowtaa/ "short"	/kowtaatar/ "shorter"	/kotaatarin/ "shortest'
/laayeq/ "capable"	/laayeqtar/ "more capable"	/laayeqtarin/ "most capable"
/chaalaak/ "shrewd"	/chaalaaktar/ "more shrewd"	/chaalaaktarin/ "most shrewd"
/qimat/ "expensive'	/qimattar/ "more expensive'	/qimattarin/ "most
/bey/ "good"	/beytat/ "better"	/beytarin/ "best"

Superlative adjectives are formed with the inflection {-in}. The exception being /besyaar/ "much," whose superlative form is /besyaari/ "most," rather than */besyaartarin/ when modifying a noun. Thus, /besyaari mardom/ means "most people" but not */besyaartarin mardom/.

Comparing Nouns Phrases (NP)

To compare two noun phrases (NPs), the comparative marker {-tar} is added to the adjective. In such constructions, the second NP is preceded by the preposition {az} "from," and followed by {kada} "than," the adjective, and a linking verb, or verb proper. Thus:

NP1 + az NP2+ kada+ADJ+tar+Be (Linking verb)/Verb Proper

Examples:

/kaabol az baghlaan kada kanlaan**tar**-as/ "Kabul is bigger than Baghlan."
/gowsht az naan kada qimattar-as/ "Meat is more expensive than bread."
/i aks az u aks kada khubtar maalum meysha/ "This picture looks better than that one,"
/ma az tu kada pashtow zyaattar meyfaamom/ "I know more Pashto than you,"
/ma az karim kada zyaat maalumaat daarom./ "I have more information than Karim."

Equal Comparison

The above examples illustrate unequal comparisons. However, there are also equal comparisons. Here, the two NPs are the same as the following examples illustrate.

Examples:

/segret **mesl-e** naswaar mozer-as/ "Smoking is as harmful as mouth snuff."
/qandaar **baraabar-e** mazaar dur-as/ "Kandahar is just as far as Mazar."
/naak **mesl-e** seyb sherin-as/ "Pears are as sweet as apples."
/karim **mesl-e** maari ushyaar-as/ "Karim is as smart as Mary."

Note that the equal words /mesl-e/ and /baraabar-e/ have the same meaning; one can be substituted for the other, and both take the Izafa. Such comparisons can be stated in a formula: **NP1+ mesl-e NP2+Adj+ Be.**

Such comparisons can also be in the negative: /seyb mesl-e angur shirin ney-s/ "Apples are not as sweet as grapes." /kaabol mesl-e jalaalabad garm ney-s/ "Kabul is not as warm as Jelalabad."

Simple and Compound Adjectives

Like verbs, adjectives are also divided into simple and compound. For example, /khosh/ "happy" is simple while /khoshqawaara/ "good looking" is compound. The reason /khoshqawaara/ is an adjective, in that it takes the comparative and superlative markers {-tar} and {-in}. Thus, / i aadam as u aadam kada khoshqawqaaratar-as/ "means "This man is more handsome than the other one." and, /u khoshqaratarin adam da enja-s/ means "He is the most handsome man here." Here are some examples of simple and compound adjectives:

Examples:

Simple	Compound
/khosh/ "like"	/khoshsowbat/ "sweet talker"
/bad/ "bad"	/badraftaar/ "bad behavior"
/bad/	/badgoftaar/ "bad-mouthed"
/kharaab/ "bad"	/kharaabkaar/ "destructive"
/teyz/ "fast"	/teyzraftaar/ "fast"
/khosh/ "like"	/khoshlebaas/ "stylish"

Derived Adjectives

Adjectives can be derived from verbs and nouns by adding derivatives. Thus:

From Verbs
By adding {**naa-**}

Present Verb stems	Adjectives
/-shenaas-/ "to know"	/naashenaas/ "unknown"
/-daar-/ "to have"	/naadaar/ "poor"

From nouns
By adding [-**daar**] "possess/own"

Nouns	Adjectives
/maza/ "taste"	/maza**daar**/ "tasty"
/paysa/ "money"	/paysa**daar**/ "rich"

/awsela/ "patience"   /awsela**daar**/ "patient"
/imaan/ "faith"   /imaandaar/ "faithful"

By adding [bey-] "without"

Nouns	Adjectives
/imaan/ "faith"	**bey**imaan/ "unfaithful"
/talim/ "education"	/**bey**talim/ "uneducated"
/saliqa/ "style"	/**bey**saliqa/ "unstylish/ disorganized"
/maanaa/ "meaning"	/**bey**maanaa/ "meaningless"
/parwaa/ "care"	/**bey**parwaa/ "careless/sloppy"
/raam/ "sympathy"	/**bey**raam/ "unsympathetic"
/taraf/ "side"	/**bey**taraf/ "neutral/indifferent"
/sewaad/ "literacy or education"	/**bey**sewaad/ "nonliterate or uneducated

By adding {-naak}

Nouns	Adjectives
/dard/ "pain"	/dard**naak**/ "painful"
/khatar/ "danger"	/khatar**naak**/ "dangerous"
/bim/ "fear"	/bim**naak**/ "fearful"
/tars/ "fear"	/tars**naak**/ "fearful"

By adding [baa-] "with"

Nouns	Adjectives
/wejdaan/ "conscience"	/**baa**wejdaan/ "conscientious"
/naamus/ "honor"	/**baa**naamus/ "honorable"
/jorat/ "courage"	/**baa**jorat/ "courageous"
/ayseyat/ "dignity"	/**baa**ayseyat/ "dignified"

By adding the past participle of the verb [-zada-] and [-kada]

Noun	Adjective
/mosibat/ "calamity"	/mosibat**zada**/ "calamity stricken"

/gham/ "sorrow" /gham**zada**/ "sorrow stricken."
/baaraan/ "rain" /baaraan**zada**/ "rain stricken"
/khod/ "self" /khod**kada**/ "self-inflicted"

By adding [-mand]

/dawlat/ "wealth" /dawlat**mand**/ "rich/wealthy"
/ezat/ "honor" /ezat**mand**/ "honorable"
/sud/ "profit" /sud**mand**/ "profitable"
/sharaafat/ "nobility" /sharaafat**mand**/ "noble"
/qodrat/ "power" /qodrat**mand**/ "powerful"

By adding [-i]

/sharaab/ "alcohol" /sharaab**i**/ "alcoholic"
/chars/ "hashish" /chars**i**/ "hashish addict"

By adding [-khowr] "eat"

/reshwat/ "bribe" /reshwat**khowr**/ "corrupt or bribe taker"
/gham/ "worry" /gham**khowr**/ "trouble shooter"

By adding [-aalud]

/khaw/ "sleep" /khwa**aalud**/ "sleepy"
/gard/ "dust" /gard**aalud**/ "dusty"

By adding [-aawar] "bring"

/dard/ "pain' /dard**aawar**/ "painful"
/sharm/ "shame" /sharm**aawar**/ "shameful"
/tasof/ "regret" /tasof**aawar**/ "regretful"
/khejaalat/ "embarrassment" /khejalat**aawar**/ "embarrassing"
/rang/ "pain/suffering" /ranj**aawar**/ "painful"

Adjective Functions

Adjectives modify nouns, verbs and function as predicates. When modifying nouns, they are said to be attributive, and when they function as subject complements, they are said to be predicative. As predicative, adjectives are used in sentences with linking verbs, /bodan/ "being" and /shodan/ "becoming,. Note that, in the following examples, Adj+Noun (#2) is emphatic whereas N+e Adj (#3) is not.

Examples:
1. /ketaab **khub**-as/ "The book is good.   **Predicative** (Noun Modifier)
2. /**khub** ketaab/ "a good book"   **Attributive** (Noun Modifier)
3. /ketaab-e **khub**/ "a good book"   **Attributive** (Noun Modifier)
4. /**khub** meysha/ "It'll be good (Literally, It becomes good)"   **Predicative**

The Adjectival Phrase

Like nouns and verbs, adjectives can have modifiers of their own. More specifically, only gradable adjectives fall in this category. In an adjectival phrase, the modifiers are adverbs of quantity and degree. An adjectival phrase consists of a modifier, and an adjective where the modifier precedes the adjective.

Examples:

1. /i ketaaab **besyaar** khub-as/	"This book is **very** good."
2. /i ketaab **besyaar** khub neys/	"This book is not very good."
3. /i ketaab **oqa** khub neys/	"This book is not **very** good."
4. /i ketaab **oqa besyaar** khub neys/	"This book is not that good."
5. /i ketaab **chandaan** khub neys/	"This book is not **very** good."
6. /i ketaab **kam-e** khub-as/	"This book is **somewhat** good."
7. /i ketaab **zyaat** khub-neys/	"This book is not **very** good."
8. /i ketaab **besyaar zyaat** khub-as/	"This book is not much better."

Here, it is important to note that: a) only gradable adjectives are modified by adverbs, b) adjectives can have two premodifiers, adverbs of quantity and degree, where the former precedes the latter (#4 and# 8); c) in the presence of /oqa/ and /chandaan/, the sentence must be negative (#3,#4, and# 5), and d) /chandaan/ and /kam-e/ cannot occur with any other premodifiers (#5 and# 6).

Chapter Summary

Adjectives belong to a class of their own. They are either stative or gradable. Most Dari adjectives are of the second category. The difference is that, gradable adjectives have the property of degrees while stative adjectives do not. The comparative marker is {-tar}, and the superlative form is made by adding {-in} to the comparative. The formula in such a comparison is: **NP1+az+ NP2+ Be**. However, Dari also has a construction for comparing equal objects where the formula is: **NP1+mesl-e NP2+Adj+Be/Verb.**

Some Dari adjectives are simple and others are compound. Adjectives can be made by adding derivatives to verbs and nouns. Adjectives can modify nouns and verbs. Finally, adjectives are modified by adverbs of degree and quantity.

Exercises

1. Are the following statements true (T) or false (F)?

    F   Most Dari adjective are stative.
    _____ An adjective can also function as an adverb.
    _____ Adjectives usually precede the noun in a noun phrase.
    _____ In comparing two objects only a linking verb (Be) is used.
    _____ The preposition /az/ "from" is used when comparing two equal objects.
    _____ The equal words used in the comparison of two equal objects always take the Izafa.

2. Translate the following into English.

    /u reshwatkhowr neys/ He is not a bribe taker.
    /nesf-e i keyka khowrd/ _____
    /i mowtar as u mowtar kada qimat-as/ _____
    /u dars-e faarsi mesl-e u dars-as/ _____
    /qandaar baraabar-e jelaalabaad garm-as/ _____
    /u mowtaraam kharaab-as/ _____
    /jelaalabaad garm-as yaa qandaar/ _____
    /aksar-e afghaanaa dawlatmand neystan/ _____
    /qimataa da baazaar yak baraabar neys/ _____
    /i chaaqu mesl-e u chaaqu teyz-as/ _____

3. Translate the following into Dari.

This tea is not very sweet. /i chaay besyaar sherin neys/
These socks are as expensive as those. _____
The majority of Afghans are very poor._____
I bought five dozens of good eggs. _____
His brother is not very intelligent. _____
My office is very close. _____
Pashto is not as easy as Dari. _____
American cars are a lot more expensive. _____
Bring me five very good cups of tea. _____
Are all of these books yours? _____

5

Adverbs and Prepositions

Introduction

This chapter is about adverbs and prepositions. We deal with adverbs first and discuss propositions later in the chapter.

Adverb is about **how, when** and **where** an action takes place. Hence they express time, manner, place, frequency, quantity, or degree. Adverbs modify verbs, nouns, and adjectives. Adverbs can function as non-phrases, phrases, and clauses. They have inflictional and derivational forms.

The following examples illustrate the various types of adverbs and how they function in a sentence.

Examples:

/**zud** raft/ "He/She/It went **fast**." — **Manner (**Verb modifier**)**

/**besyaar** qimat-as/ "It's **very** expensive." — **Quantity** (Adjective modifier)

/**emrowz** raft/ "He/She left **today**." — **Time** (Sentence modifier)

/ketaab **sar-e meyz**-as/ "The book is **on the table**." — **Place** (Predicative)

/**baaz-e wakht** sinomaa meyrom/ "**Sometimes** I go to the movies." — **Frequency** (Sentence modifier)

/qolfa **kat-e keli** waaz kad/ "He/She opened the lock **with a key**." — **Manner (**Noun modifier**)**

/**ar rowz** maktab meyra/ "He goes home **everyday**. — **Frequency** (Sentence modifier**)**

/**shawaana** dars meykhaana/ "He studies **at night**." — **Frequency (**Verb modifier**)**

/az taraf-e rowz khaw meysha/ "He sleeps during the day."

Frequency (Verb modifier)

/zud zud raa meyra/ "He walks **fast**."

Manner (Verb modifier)

Comparison of Adverbs

Like adjectives, adverbs also take the comparitive marker {-tar} as the following examples illustrate.

Examples:

1. /mowtar az baaysekel kada **teyztar** meyra/ "A car goes **faster** than a bike."
2. **/teyztar** borrow/ "Go **faster**."
3. **/teyz teyz** borrow/ "Go **faster**."
4. /lotfan **aastatar** gap bezan/ "Please speak **more slowly**."
5. /lotfan **aastaa aastaa** gap bezan/ "Please speak **more slowly**."

Note that #2 and #3 as well as #5 and #6 are paraphrases in that, they have the same meaning. Also, it is important to note that, when an adverb is repeated, it does not take the comparative marker (#3 and #6).

Derived Adverbs

Adverbs can be derived from nouns.

By adding {-aki}

Noun	Adverb
/sowb/ "morning"	/sowb**aki**/ "in the morning"
/chaasht/ "noon"	/chaasht**aki**/ "at noon"
/shaw/ "night"	/shaw**aki**/ "at night"
/rowz/ "day"	/rowz**aki**/ "daily"
/maa/ "month"	/maa**gaki**/ "monthly"
/afta/ "week"	/afta**gaki**/ "weekly"
/saal/ "year"	/saal**aki**/ "annually/yearly"
/nafar/ "individual"	/nafar**aki**/ "individually"
/khaana/ "house"	/khaana**gaki**/ "on a house-to-house basis"
/wakht/ "time"	/wakht**aki**/ "early"

/qarn/ "century"   /qarn**aki**/ "century wise"

Note that, {-aki} has two allomorphs: {-aki} after a consonant and {-gaki} after a vowel.

By adding {-aana}

Noun	Adverb
/rowz/ "day"	/rowz**aana**/ "daily"
/chaasht/ "noon"	/chaasht**aana**/ "at noon"
/shaw/ "night"	/shaw**aana**/
/saal/ "year"	/saal**aana**/ "yearly"
/maa/ "month"	/maa.**aana**/ "monthly"
/beytaraf/ "unbiased/ indifferent"	/beytaraf**aana**/ "indifferently/ unbiased"

It is worth noting that, some of the above adverbs of frequency are derived from phrases. For example, non-phrases such as /rowzaki/, or /rowzaana/ "daily" is the contracted form of the phrase /az taraf-e rowz/ "during the day," or /ar rowz/ "every day." The long forms are usually emphatic while the contracted ones are not. As the following illustrate, some of the long forms are noun (#2, #3, and #4), and others are propositional phrases (#1 and #5).

Examples:

	Phrase (Emphatic)	Non-phrase (Non Emphatic)
1.	/az taraf-e shaw/ "during the evening/night"	/shawaana/ or /shawaki/ "nightly."
2.	/ar saal/ "every year"	/saalaana/ "yearly"
3.	/ar maa/ "every month"	/maaaana/ "monthly"
4.	/ar afta/ "every week"	/aftagaki/ "weekly"
5.	/az taraf-e rowz/ "during the day"	/rowzaana/ or /rowzaki/ "daily"

Adverbs of Time

Time adverbials can also be used as non-phrases (single words), phrases, or even clauses.

Examples:

/**emrowz** aamad/ "He/She came today." **Noun Phrase (NP)**

/maari **az amrikaa**-s/ "Mary is from America." **Prepositional Phrase (PP)**

/**wakht-e ke aamad** ma khaana nabodom/ "When he/she came I was not home." **Clause** (Sentence modifier)

/**saat-e do baja** meyra/ "He leaves at two o'clock." **NP**

/**wakht** raft/ "He left early." **Non-phrase**

/**ba shedat** jowaab daad/ "He responded harshly." **PP**

Adverbs of Manner

Manner adverbs modify verbs as non-phrases or phrases.

Examples:

/teyz raft/	"He/She went fast."	Non-phrase
/ba tizi raft/	"He/She went very fast."	Phrase
/da mowtar khaana raft/	"He went home in a car."	Phrase
/wakhttar aamad/	"He came earlier.	Non-phrase
/fawran raft/	"He left immediately."	Non-phrase
/dafatan goft/	"He said immediately."	Non-phrase
/zud pasaamad/	"He came back fast."	Non-phrase
/pasaan raft/	"He left late."	Non-phrase
/naawakht rasid/	"He arrived late."	Non-phrase
/ba tizi goft/	"He said immediately."	Phrase
/deyr maatel kad/	"He waited long."	Non-phrase
/ba aastaayi goft/	"He said slowly."	Phrase
/aasta borrow/	"Go slow."	Non-phrase
/aastaa aastaa meryraft/	"He was going very slowly or low."	
/besyaar zud zud arakat meykona/	"He moves too fast."	

Some other manner adverbs that behave like {teyz} are: {aastaa} "slow," {aaraam} "quiet/slow/soft," {sost} "weak/slow," and {zud} "fast/quick." Note also that, as mentioned earlier, some adverbs of manner can be repeated to express higher or lower degree as in /zud zud gap meyzana/ "He speaks very fast or faster." And /besyaar zud zud/ means "faster."

Adverbs of Place

Adverbs of place too, can be non-phrases (single words), phrases or even clauses. They can function as subject or predicate, and can modify nouns and clauses.

Examples:

/ma **khaana** raftom/ "I went home."	**Non-phrase** (Sentence modifier).
/kaabol **da afghaanestaan**-as/ "Kabul is in Afghanistan."	**Phrase** (Predicative)
/ketaab **sar-e meyz**-as/ "The book on the table belongs to me."	**Phrase** (Noun modifier)
/**jaay-e ke tu miri** dur-as/ "The place you are going is far."	**Clause** (Subject)

Adverbs of Degree

/u **besyaar teyz meyra**/	"He goes **very** fast."
/i **kam-e** teyz meykhaana/	"He reads **a bit** faster."
/ma **oqa** teyz nameyrom/	"I don't go **that (much)** fast."
/u **chandaan** teyz gap nameyzana/	"He doesn't speak **that (much)** fast."

Note that, the adverb /kam-e/ "a little/ a bit" is derived from the adjective /kam/ "less/little," and takes the Izafa when used as an adverb. Additionally, when /oqa/ and /chandaan/ mean "that much," the sentence is always in the negative.

Adverbs of Frequency

Adverbs of frequency include /ameysha/ "always," /baaz-e wakht/yagaan wakht/ "sometimes," /baaz-e wakhtaa/ "some of the times," /omuman/ "usually," / arwakht/ "all the time," /nodratan/ "rarely," and /eychwakht/ abadan/ "never," as the following illustrates:

Examples:

1. /ma **ameysha** yak pyaala kaafi meykhorom/ "I **always** drink a cup of coffee."

2. /**baaz-e wakhtaa** karim da rasturaan naan meykhora/ "Karim **sometimes** eats at a restaurant."
3. /yak mosolmaan baayad **eychwakht** sharaab nakhora/ "A Muslim should n**ever** drink alcohol."
4. /ma **yagaan wakht** kaafi meykhorom/ "I **sometimes** drink coffee."
5. /ma **baaz-e wakht** khabaraara gowsh meykonom/ "I listen to the news some of the time."
6. /u **abadan** i kaara nameykona/ "He **never** does this."
7. /**fawran** tu baayd peysh-e daaktar bori/ "You should go to the doctor immediately."
8. /**ejaalatan** yak nafar mowtarwaan kefaayat meykona/ "One driver is enough **for now.**"

It is worth noting that, most adverbs of frequency are phrases rather than non-phrases. Additionally, /baaz-e/ can be used either with a singular or plural noun, but not /yagaan/. Thus /baaz-e wakht/, or /baaz-e wakhtaa (#2 and #4), but not */yagaan wakhtaa/. Also, with /abadan/ or /eychwakht/ "never," the sentence must be in the negative (#3 and #6). Furthermore, since this is different from English, it may be problematic to a native speaker of English. Additionally, frequency words ending in /-an/ (#6, #7, and #8) are Arabic loan words. Also, adverbs ending with /-an/ are loan words from Arabic: /fawran/, /dafatan/,/ ejalatan/, /omuman/. Finally, like other adverbs, adverbs of frequency are mobile, and can be moved in a sentence; a phenomenon different from English in which, such frequency words always follow the verb to be, and precede other verbs. Compare "He **is** always on time," and "He always **watches** cowboy movies."

Prepositions

A preposition is defined as "a function word that typically combines with a noun to form a phrase which is usually a modification or predication." [6] Prepositions in Dari can be free or bound, simple, or derived.

Dari prepositions are inflected (bound) and free. The majority of Dari prepositions are inflected, and they are derived from nouns and adjectives (#5, # 6 below). The inflection used is the Izafa that connects the word modified to the modifier. In /sar-e meyz/ "on the table," for example, the preposition {sar-e} has the Izafa, {-e}. Perhaps, {da} "in/at" {taa} "to/until" (#1, #4 and #11), and {ba} "to" (#11) are the only free prepositions in the language. Some of the inflected prepositions, however, behave as both free and bound (#3 and #10).

---

[6]   Merriam Webster's Collegiate Dictionary, 981.

Examples:

1. /ketaab **da** khaana-s/ "The book is at home."   Free
2. /ketaab **az** ma-s/   Free
3. /**az** kaabol **taa** ghazni cheqa raa-s / "What is the distance between Kabul and Ghazni?"   Free
4. /**taa** panj baja khalaas meysha/ "It will be finished by five o'clock."   Free
5. /**sar-e** meyz-as/ "It's on the table."   Bound
6. /**nezdik-e** daftar-as/ "It's near the office."   Bound
7. /ketaaba **barem** daad/ "He/She gave the book to me."   Bound
8. /**kat-e** ma borow/ "Go with me."   Bound
9. /**kat-e-sh** gap bezan/ "Talk to him/her."   Bound
10. /ketaaba **azesh** gereftom/ "I took the book from him."   Bound
11. /**ba** ma eych marbut ney-s/ "It has nothing to do with me."   Free

Suffixed Prepositions

Prepositions are also suffixed with possessive pronouns as the following examples illustrate:

1. /ketaaba **azem** gereft/ "He/She took the book from me."
2. /ketaaba **barem** daadan/ "They gave me the book."
3. /ma **saresh** paysa qarz daarom/ "He/She owns me money."
4. /ma **amraaytan** meyrom/ "I go with you."
5. /**kateshaan** chi kadi/ "What did you do **with them?**"

It is important to note that, the suffixed prepositions are the contracted (nonemphatic) forms as the following examples explain.

	Long Form	Contracted Forms
1	/bar-e ma/ "for me"	/bare-m/ "for me"
2	/bar-e maa/ "for us"	/bar-e-maa/ "for us"
3	/bar-e tu/ "for you"	/bar-et/ "for you" (singular) 1"
4	/bar-e shomaa/ "for you (plural)	/ar-e-taan/ "for you (plural)
5	/bar-e u/ "for him/her/it"	/bar-esh/ "for him/her/ it"
6	/bar-e unaa/ "for them"	/bar-e-shaan/ "for them"

Other prespositions that behave like /bar/ are:/sar-e/ "on," /amraa/ "with," /kat/ "with," /nezdik/ "near," /rubru/ "front," /pas/ "back," /az/ "from," and others. Note that in the long and contracted forms both the Izafa is present.

Addition, Exception and Restriction

Dari prepositions can be used to express addition, exception, and restriction.

Addition

Some prepositions indicate addition or inclusion. Thus:

/**amraa-ye** ma raft/ means "He went **with** me."
/**ba shomul-e** ma kol-e famil mariz shod/ means "The entire family became sick, **including** me."

Exception

The opposite of addition is exception. Adverbs of exception are also expressed by prepositions. Thus:
/**ghayr-e** ma kolagi raftan/ "Everybody went **except** me."
/**bedun-e** ma raftan/ "They left **without** me."
/**bedun-e** barq nameysha/ "It can't be done **without** electricity."
/**bedun-e** feshaar-e khaarej reshwat az afghaanestaan gom nameysha/ "**Without** foreign pressure, corruption cannot be uprooted from Afghanistan."

Note that most words of addition and exception take the Izafa.

Restriction

Restriction involves a combination of negative meaning with the idea of exception. Thus:
/**tanaa** chaay khowrd/ "He **only** had tea."
/**faqat** panj daqiqa gap zad / "He **only** spoke for five minutes."
/**serf** yak rowz ba rowza maanda / "**Only** one day left for Ramazan."

Derived Prepositions

As the following examples illustrate, bound prepositions are derived from nouns and adjectives:

Examples

Noun Preposition

/sar/ "top, head"	/**sar-e** meyz/	"on the table"
/robru/ "straight"	/**robru-ye** khaana/	"in front of the "house"
/amraa/ "companion"	/**amraa-ye** beraadar/	"with "brother"
/moqaabel/ "across"	/**moqaabe-e** khaana/	"across from the house"
/taraf/ "toward"	/**taraf-e** jelaalaabaad/	"toward Jalalabad"
/zeyr/ "under"	/**zeyr-e** ketaab/	"under the book"
/bar/ "side"	/**bar-e** ma/	"to me"
/sun/ "toward, direction"	/**sun-e** ma/	

Adjective Preposition

/nezdik/ "near"	/**nezdik-e** khaana/ "near the house"
/baalaa/ "high"	/**baalaa-ye** meyz/

The above prepositional phrases can be contracted with the use of genitive pronouns. It is worth noting, however, that only those phrases that involve bound prepositions undergo this rule. For example, /da khaana/ "in the house," does not have a contracted form because /da/ is used only as a non-phrase.

Examples:

Long (Emphatic)	Contracted (Nonemphatic)
/bar-e ma/ "for /to me"	/barem/
/nezdik-e karim/ "near Karim"	/nezdikesh/ "near him"
/sar-e ketaab/ "on the book"	/saresh/ "on it"
/moqaabel-e khaana/ "in front of the house"	/moqaabelesh/ "in front of it"
/sar-e too/ "on you"	/saret/ "on you"

By adding {ba-}

Noun	Adverb
/khubi/ "wellness"	/**ba**bakhubi/ "well"

/kharaabi/ "badness"   /**ba**kharaabi/ "badly"

/sharmi/ "shame"   /**ba**sharmi/ "shamefully"

/zudi/ "speed"   /**ba**zudi/ "fast"

Prepositions and Gerunds.

Among the bound prepositions, /**sar-e**/ "on/ at," when used with a gerund, indicate an action in progress, while the use of /**bar-e**/ "for/to" expresses purpose. The following illustrates these functions:

/meymaanaa **sar-e khowrdan**-astan/	"The guests are eating." (Literally. The guests are at eating.)
/ma **sar-e raftan** bodom ke karim aamad/	"I was leaving when Karim came."
/ma **sar-e khaandan**-astom/	"I'm reading."
/ma **sar-e dars dadan**-astom/	"I'm teaching."
/ma **sar-e goftan** bodom ke teylefun aamad/	"I was talking when the phone rang."
/naan **bar-e khowrdan**-as/	"Food/Bread is for eating."
/saabun **bar-e paak kadan**-as/	"Soap is for cleaning."
/paysa **bar-e kharch kadan**-as/	"Money is for spending/The purpose of money is to spend."
/ketaab **bar-e khaandan**-as/	"Books are for reading."
/**bar-e naan khowrdan** rasturaan meyrom/	"I'm going to the restaurant to eat."
/kaar kadan **bar-e maash**-as/	"Working is for purpose of getting a salary."
/mowtar **bar-e safar** kadan-as/	"Cars are for traveling."

As it was pointed out in the chapter on verbs, unlike English, Dari does not have present progressive tense. Hence, it makes use of other mechanisms to express an action in progress. Apart from the use of the preposition /sar-e/ + Gerund, Dari makes use of the adverb /**deydey**/ "while," "at the moment," or "continuously," "right now," to express an action in progress.

Examples:

1. /**deydey** naan meykhoran/	"They are eating **right now**."
2. /**deydey** myaayan/	"They **keep coming**."
3. /**deydey** jang meykonan/	"They are fighting **at the moment**."

Prepositional Phrases

Prepositional phrases function as adverbs of time, place, and manner, direct objects, predicates, and noun, and verb modifiers.

Examples:

/karim **az kaabol**-as/ "Karim is **from** Kabul."	**Predicate (place)** (see earlier note on dots)
/ketaab-e **sar-e meyz**/ "The book **on** the table."	**Noun Modifier (place)**
/qolfa **kat-e keli** waaz kad/ "He/She opened the lock **with** a key."	**Verb Modifier (instrument)**
/mowtara **bar-e ma** meyta/ "He/She is giving the car **to** me."	**Indirect Object**
/ketaaba **az ma** gereft/ "He/She took the book **from me**."	**Indirect Object**
/ma **da sarweys** raftom/ "I went by bus."	**Verb Modifier (means)**
/meymaanaa **sar-e naan**-astan/ "The guests are eating."	**Predicate (place)**

Chapter Summary

Adverbs too, belong to a distinct class. Adverbs express time, place, manner, degree, and they function as modifiers of verbs, adjectives, nouns, and clauses. An adverb can be a non-phrase, a phrase, or a clause. There are simple, compound, and derived.

Prepositions also make a class of their own. Like adverbs, they have grammatical meaning, and function as non-phrases or phrases. Dari prepositions are bound or free. Bound prepositions take the Izafa, and they are much more numerous than free prepositions. Bound prepositions are derived from nouns and verbs.

Unlike English, prepositions take the possessive suffix. Some bound prepositions such as /sar-e/ "on," when used with a gerund, express an action in progress; the addition of /deydey/ serves the same purpose. Finally, some prepositions are used as phrases (long) and non-phrases (contracted). However, only phrases with bound prepositions can be contracted.

Exercises

1. Are the following statements True or False?

F The position of time adverbials is fixed in Dari.
_____ Adverbs of frequency can have long and short forms.
_____ Most Dari prepositions are free.
_____ Some prepositions are derived from adjectives.
_____ Bound prepositions require the Izafa.
_____ An adverb modifying a noun can be non-phrases.
_____ Only time adverbials can function as a clause.
_____ /taa/ and /az/ are adverbs.

2. Translate the following into English.

/ki besyaar naan meykhora/	"Who eats a lot?"
/maam paysa nadaarom/	_____
/ar afta sefaarat namiri?/	_____
/cheraa rowzaky khaw mishi/	_____
/maa maaaana maash megereym/	_____
/malem-e maa emrowz mariz-as/	_____
/ma aale naan namekhorom/	_____
/i bachaa da sarweys khaana nameyran/	_____
/da i senf chand nafar-as/	_____
/ketaab-e karim da kojaa-s/	_____
/az taraf-e chaasht kabaab meykhora/	_____
/ki besyaar zud zud naan meykhora/	_____
/englisi gap zadan bar-e ma aasaantar-as/	_____
/naan bar-e meymaanaa-s/	_____

3. Translate the following into Dari.

He reads during the day.	/rowzaana ketaab meykhaana/
He stirred the tea with a spoon.	_____
Every year I go to America.	_____
Everyone speaks English but me.	_____
He immediately left the room.	_____

He should come right away.   ———————————

A radio is for listening.   ———————————

Do you usually talk to her?   ———————————

I'm eating breakfast now.   ———————————

Are you from Kandahar?   ———————————

What time does the bus come?   ———————————

This tea is not very good.   ———————————

6

Clauses

Introduction

The last four chapters dealt with phrases, verbs, nouns, adjectives, adverbs, and prepositions. This chapter is about clauses. More specifically, it describes sentence and clause types. A sentence expresses a "complete thought," and stands by itself

(independent). Structurally, a sentence has at least a finite verb, and in the case of a linking verb (/budan/ and /shodan/), it also includes a noun phrase, and an adjectival phrase as complement. A clause on the other hand, does not occur by itself; it is dependent. As it will be clear, sentences are simple (basic), complex, and compound.

Simple, Complex and Compound Sentences

The largest grammatical constituent is the sentence, and the smallest is the word. In between, there are phrases and clauses. For example, in the English sentence, *The man bought a car,* the immediate constituents are **the man (Noun phrase)** and **bought a car (Verb phrase)**. The immediate constituents of **the man (NP)** and **bought a car (VP)** are **the** and **man** and **bought (V),** and **a car (NP) respectively.** The immediate constituents of the NP are **a (DET)** and **car (N).** Thus, the smallest constituents of the above sentence are **The+man + bought+a+car,** which cannot be analyzed into further constituents. All NPs, VPs, AdjPs, AdvPs, and PrepPs have a nucleus or head which is obligatory, and dependents, or modifiers which are optional.

The verb functions as head in a verb phrase with or without modifiers (dependents). The constituents of a verb phrase determine the kernel or basic sentence patterns in a language. In a basic sentence, all the constituents are obligatory.

Basic Sentence Patterns

The obligatory constituents of Dari verb phrase are the following:

1. /jaan az amrikaa-s/ "John is from America." **NP+Adverbial Phrase+Be**
2. /u malem-as/ "He/She is a teacher." **NP1+NP1+Be**
3. /u khosh-as/ "He/She is happy." **NP+Adjective+Be**
4. /u meyra/ "He/She goes/is going." **NP+Verb** intr.
5. /karim kabaaba khosh daara/ "Karim likes kabobs." **NP1+ NP2+Verb**-mono-transitive
6. /karim ketaaba mara daad/ "Karim gave me the book." **NP1+NP2+NP3+Verb**-di-transitive
7. /i khub meysha/ "(It) sounds good/It will be good." **NP+Adj+Verb- shodan** (to become)
8. /karim malem meysha/ "(He/She) becomes a teacher." **NP1+NP1+Verb-shudan**
9. /karzay abdulaara wazir moqarar kad / "Karzai appointed Abdullah minister." **NP1+NP2+NP2+Verb**-moqarar

The presence of subject in all the above sentences is optional, because the suffixes in the verb indicate the subject; a separate subject is used for emphasis. Note also that, the NPs in (2) and (8) refer to the same person. Similarly, in (9), the NPs in the predicate refer to the same person. Modifiers can be added to the NPs and VPs in the above sentences. Since these modifiers are optional unless for emphasis, they are not part of the basic or kernel sentence or patterns of Dari, which are summarized in the following formulas:

Type #1. NP + AdvP+Linking (budan)
/karim khaana-s/ "Karim is home."

Type #2. NP1+NP1+Linking (budan)
/karim malem-as/ "Karim is a teacher."

Type #3. NP+Adjective+Linking (budan)
/karim mariz-as/ "Karim is sick."

Type #4. NP1+NP2+ VP.mono-transitive
/karim khaana kharid/ "Karim bought a house."

Type #5. NP1+NP2+NP3+ VP.di-transitive
/karim mara ketaab daad/ "Karim gave me a book."

Type #6 NP+Adj. +Linking (shodan)
/karim mariz shod/ "Karim became sick."

Type #7. NP1+NP1+Linking (shodan)
/karim malem shod/ "Karim became a teacher."

Type #8. NP+VP-intransitive
/karim raft/ "Karim left."

Type#9. NP1+NP2+NP2+Verb-moqarar
/karim mara malem moqarar kad/ "Karim made me a teacher."

Among the above sentence patterns, #9 is not as common as the rest. The only other verb that behaves like /moqarar/ is /tayin/, which also means "to appoint."

Declarative and Interrogative Sentences

There are two types of interrogatives: open and closed. The former is also referred to as W-H questions in English. There are two types of questions: open and closed. Closed interrogatives, also called yes-no questions, requiring no explanation. Hence the term "closed." Closed interrogatives are made by a rising intonation while open interrogatives call for interrogative words such as /ki/ "who," /cheraa/ "why," /bar-e chi/ "what for," /che wakht/ "when," /kojaa/ "where," /chi/ "what," /chetowr/ "how," /cheqa/, or /cheqadar/ "how much," /chand/ "how many," and so on. Like English, open interrogatives require a falling intonation. A declarative clause has a falling intonation and does not require any interrogative word.

Examples:

/ketaab qimat-as?	"Is the book expensive?"	**Closed**
/**cheraa** karzay estefaa nameykona/	"Why doesn't Karzai resign?"	**Open**
/**bar-e chi** khaana rafti/	"Why did you go home?"	**Open**

/**chi** gofti/	"What did you say?"	**Open**
/khaanara kharidi?/	"Did you buy the house?"	**Closed**
/**bar-e chi** dars nameykhaani/	"Why don't you study?"	**Open**
/kaar khalaas shod?/	"Is the work done?"	**Closed**

Complex and Compound Sentences

Basic or kernel sentences can be combined to generate complex and compound sentences. In a complex sentence, one sentence is embedded into another (embedding), whereas in a compound sentence, two basic sentences are conjoined (conjoining). In embedding, one sentence becomes part of another. In the following, (1) is embedded into (2) generating the complex sentence (3).

(1) /ketaab englisi-s/ "The book is English."
(2) /ketaab az ma-s/ "The book belongs to me."
(3) /ktaab-e englisi az ma-s/ "The English book belongs to me/is mine."

Restrictive and nonrestrictive clauses, to be discussed shortly, are examples of embedding. So are noun clauses (NC). To give another example, the complex sentence/ketaab-e kalaan qimat-as/ "The big book is expensive," is generated from two simple sentences: (1) / ketaab kalaan-as/ and (2) / ketaab qimat-as/ "The book is expensive," where (1) is embedded into (2) generating /ketaab-e kalaan qimat-as/ (3).

In a compound sentence, on the other hand, two sentences are conjoined, using the coordinating conjunctions {wa} "and" or {yaa} "or." In conjoining, the sentences joined together have equal weight. In the following, (1) and (2) are conjoined to generate the compound sentence (3).

(1) /khaana raftom/ "I went home."
(2) /naan khowrdom/ "I ate."
(3) /khaana raftom-o-naan khowrdom/ "I went home and ate."

The conjunction "wa" has three allomorphs: {**wa**}, {**o**} or {**wo**}. {**wa**} is used between pauses and it can be emphatic. The allomorph {-o-} is used, if the preceding sound is a consonant, and {-wo-} when it is a vowel. Thus, /qalam-**o**-kaaghaz/ means "pen and paper" but /chawki-**wo**-meyz/ means "chair and table." If more than two sentences are conjoined, pauses are also employed. Thus, the compound sentence / ma khaana raftom, naan khowrdom wa akhbaar khaandom/ means "I went home, ate dinner, and read the newspaper." Note that here commas indicate pauses.

Restrictive and Nonrestrictive Clauses

There are two kinds of relative clauses: restrictive and nonrestrictive. They both modify a noun in an NP in almost all of its functions.

Examples:

(1) /ketaab-e ke sar-e meyz-as az ma-s/ "The book that is on the table is mine." (Restrictive)
(2) /ketaab, ke **beytarin rafiq-e ensaan-as,** da tamaam-e ketaabforush-ya paydaa meysha/ "Books, which are man's best friend, are found in all bookstores." (Nonrestrictive)

In a restrictive clause or a relative clause such as (1) above, the information in the clause is restricted to the noun it modifies, and it does not refer to the entire class. In other words, only the book on the table is mine, not all books. Note also that, in a restrictive clause (RC), the Izafa is present. The construction in (2), on the other hand, is nonrestrictive because it refers to the entire class (i.e., all books—nonrestrictive). That is to say, all books are man's best friend not just the one mentioned here. Reduced forms of the subject NPs in #s 1, and 2 are respectively, /ketaab-e sar-e meyz az ma-s/ and /ketaab, beytarin rafiq-e ensaan/. Note that unlike (1), in sentence (2), the noun /ketaab/, and its modifier beytarin rafiq-e ensaan/ are the same. That is why such constructions are also called oppositions or topic-comment clauses. Like relative clauses, opposition clauses can be restrictive, nonrestrictive, or explicit as the following examples illustrate.

1. /karim-**e najaar**/	"Karim the carpenter"	**Restrictive Opposition**
2. /karim, **rafiq-e ma**/	"Karim, my friend"	**Nonrestrictive Opposition**
3. /baarak owbaamaa **yaa rayis-e jamur-e amrikaa**/	"Barack Obama or president of the United States"	**Explicit Opposition**
4. /towbarkolowz **yaa maraz-e sel**/	"TB or lung cancer"	**Explicit Opposition**
5. /eslaam, **din-e mardom-e afghaanestaan**/		**Nonrestrictive Opposition**
6. /karim-**e deragi**/ "Karim the addicted"		**Restrictive Opposition**

| 7. /daaktar entezaar, **ostaad-e powantun-e kaabol**/ | "Dr. Entezar, professor at Kabul University" | **Nonrestrictive Opposition** |
| 8. /kaabol **yaaney paytakht-e afghaanestaan**/ | "Kabul or the capital of Afghanistan" | **Explicit Opposition** |

Note that, the above opposition constructions are reduced clauses. For example /karim-e najaar/, is the reduced form of /karim ke najaar-as/ which means "Karim who is a carpenter."

Comment Phrases and Clauses

Apart from oppositions, there are also other types of comment clauses. Let us look at the following examples:

1. /**ba fekr-e ma**, kaabol maghbul-s/ "**In my opinion**, Kabul is pretty."
2. /**ba nazar-e ma**, u khub aadam neys-s/ **In my view**, he's not a good person."
3. /**ba esaab-e ma**, do sad kam-as/ "**In my calculation**, it is two hundred less."
4. /**ba aqid-ey ma**, i kaar ghalat-as/ "**In my view**, this is wrong."

Note that, the above prepositional phrases are contracted forms. In other words, they are derived from complete sentences. Thus:

Long	Short
/ma fekr meykonom/ "I think."	**/ba fekr-e ma/** "In my thinking (idea)
/i nazar-e ma-s/ "This is my view/opinion."	**/ba nazar-e ma/** "In my view"
/i esaab-e ma-s/ "This is my calculation."	**/ba esaab-e ma/** "In my calculation"
/i aqid-ey ma-s/ "This is my belief."	**/ba aqid-ey ma/** "In my view/belief"

Some other expressions used as comments are: /ba ebaar-ey dega/ "in other words," /bar alaawa/ "In addition," /bar aks/ "On the contrary," /ba raasti / "in reality/fact," /albata/ "of course," /aga az ma porsaan koni/ "If you ask me," / aga ma eywaz-e tu baashom/ "If I were you," /aga gap-e mara meshnawi/ "If you want my advice," /aga raasesha porsaan koni/ "to tell the truth," /az taraf-e dega/ "on the other hand,"/belaakhera/ "finally," /da aakherin talil/ "in the final analysis," /amchonaan/ "similarly," /dega i ke/ "additionally," /ghayr-e az u/ "in addition," and /awal i ke/ "to begin with/first."

Cleft Clauses

Still another type of Dari clause is cleft (split). Cleft clauses require linking verbs. In cleft transformation, a simple sentence is split into two to indicate contrast or emphasis. For example, /karim khaana kharid / "Karim bought a house," can be split into two clauses in a complex sentence: /i karim bud ke khaana kharid/ "It was Karim who bought the house." Note the use of {i} "it" at the beginning of the cleft transformation. To generate a cleft sentence, {i} {budan}, and {ke} are added to the first clause, and the other clause following {ke} is the rest of the simple sentence. Thus:

NP1+NP2+Verb/ becomes **/i +NP1+Link+ke+NP1+ NP2-Verb**

In the following pairs, the first sentence (a) is transformed into cleft (b). Note that, the verb in the simple sentence can either be transitive (1 and 2) or intransitive (3).

Pair #1. a)/Karim ar shaw taa naawakht dars meykhaana/ "Karim studies until late every night." b)/i karim-as ke arshaw dars meykhaana/ "It is Karim who studies until late every night."

Pair #2. a)/taalebaa mardom-e beygonaara mekosha/ "The Taliban kills innocent people." b)/i taalebaa-s ke mardom-e begonaara mekosha/ "It is the Taliban who kills innocent people."

Pair #3. a)/adisan barqa ekheteraa kad/ "Edison invented electricity." b)/i adisan bud ke barqa ekhteraa kad/ "It was Edison who invented electricity."

Noun Clauses

A noun clause (NC) replaces an NP in a sentence. In Dari, a NC functions as object of a verb (1, 2, 3, 4, 5, and 6) or as complement with a linking verb (7 and 8). Noun clauses are highlighted in the following:

Examples:

(1)/didom **ke karim khaana raft/** "I saw **Karim going home.**" **NP (Object) Verb**

(2)/goftom **ke beraadarem da melal-e mutaed kaar meykona/** "I said **that my brother works at the United Nations.**" **NP (Object)**

(3)/shonidom **ke beraadaret aarusi kad**/ "I heard **that your brother got married.**"	NP (Object)
4./meyfaamom **ke da afghaanestaan amneyat ney-s**/ "I know **that there is no security in Afghanistan.**"	NP (Object)
(5)/mara goft **ke emrowz aasmaan saaf-as**/ "He told me **that the sky is clear today.**"	
(6)/meykhaayom **ke khaana borom**/ "I want to go home."	NP (Object)
(7)/dorost ney-s **ke ma pashtowzobaan-astom**/ It is not true **that I'm a Pashto speaker.**"	NP (Complement)
(8)/khub mesha **ke khaana bori**/ "It is better **that you go home.**"	NP (Complement)
(9) /i ke karim dars kaar meykona khub-s. "That Karim has a job is good."	NP (subject)

Note that, the main verbs in (1) through (5) are transitive requiring an object. The fact that these clauses can be replaced by {-esh} "it," indicates that they are NCs. In other words, /didom ke karim khaana raft/ can be reduced to /didomesh/ "I saw it." "Here, {-esh} "it" replaces the NC /ke karim khaana raft/. Note also that unlike English, the NC in (6) is predicative. Occasionally, a NC is also used as subject as in (9). Finally, the clause introducer, {ke} "that" is obligatory in such constructions. That is why, such clauses can be called ke-clauses. This {ke} should not be confused with the pronoun {ke} "who/ which/ that" in relative clauses, discussed earlier or the {ke} "when/while" in time clauses to be discussed shortly, such as /ma ke aamadom, da khaana kas nabud/ "When I came nobody was home." It is important to keep these different {ke} constructions in mind.

Causative Clauses

A causative clause is a NC that expresses cause or reason.

Examples:
/peysh-e daaktar meyrom **ke mariz-astom**/ "I'm going to the doctor because I'm sick."
/enja byaa **ke kaaret daarom**/ "Come here **because I need you.**"
/byaa **ke baret teylefun-as**/ "Come (here) **because there is a call for you.**"
/esteraaat meykonom **ke manda-stom**/ "I'm resting **because I'm tired.**"

The clause introducer /ke/ is a reduced form of /cheraa ke/ "because of."

Conditional Clauses

Examples:

1. /**aga** tu miri, maam meyrom/ "**If** you go, I'll go too."
2. /**aga** tu bori, maam meyrom/ "**If** you go, I may go too."
3. /**aga** tu rafti, maam meyrom/ "**If** you go, I would go too."
4. /**aga** tu meyrafti, maam meyraftom/ "**If** you went, I would go too."

In the above sentences, (1) is most likely to happen (least contrary to fact) while (3) is least likely to happen (most contrary to fact). The degree of likelihood depends on the verb stem and the prefixes. Thus, (1) is more likely to happen than (2) because the latter has the optative {bo-}. Both (1) and (2) are more likely to happen than (3) because of the presence of the present verb stem in (1) and (2), and the past verb stem in (3).

Active and Passive Voice

Passive voice is derived from active. In passive voice, the emphasis is on the action, or the receiver of the action. The performer of the action (the agent) is not as important. For an active clause to undergo the passive transformation, the verb must be transitive and there must be an object or a receiver of the action. In other words, there needs to be two different noun phrases (NPs), where the first noun is the subject of the sentence, and the second one is the object of the verb. Unlike English, a separate noun as the subject (doer of the action) is not required (optional) n Dari, as it is attached to the verb. To convert a Dari active sentence into passive, the object is moved to the beginning, and the past participle form of the verb plus /shod/ "became," or /meysha/ "become" are added, depending on whether the verb is in the past or present.

Examples:

Active	Passive
(NP1)+ NP2+Verb mono-transitive	**NP2 Past Participle+shodan (to become)**
/ketaaba mebenom/ "I see the book."	/ketaab dida meysha/ "The book is seen."
/naana mekhorom/ "I eat the bread/meal."	/naan khowrda meysha/ "The bread/meal is (being) eaten."
/nana aawordan/ "They brought the meal."	/naan aworda shod/ "The meal was brought."

/darakhtaara meykanan/ "They take the tree out of the ground." /darakht kanda meysha/ "The tree is being taken out from the ground."

Direct and Indirect Speech

In direct speech, the exact words of the speaker are reported without adding or changing any words. In indirect speech, on the other hand, some words are added, and some are changed, but the meaning of the reported speech is maintained. To give an example from English, "Mary said, "I am sick," is direct while "Mary said that she was sick" is indirect. Note that, in the indirect, "I" was changed to "she," and "is" to "was," and the word "that" was added.

Neither Dari nor Pashto allows indirect speech. This causes problems when indirect speech from English is translated into Dari. The translation of "Mary said that she was sick," into */maari goft ke u mariz bud/ is inaccurate because in Dari, /u / "she" cannot refer to Mary but only to a person other than "Mary. Hence, the accurate translation of the above indirect speech into Dari would be to convert it into direct speech, and translate into: /maari goft ke ma mariz-astom/. This mistake is constantly made in the British Broadcasting Corporation (BBC), Voice of America (VOA), and news agencies that translate indirect speeches into Dari or Pashto. Nouns and verbs can be borrowed from a foreign language but not grammatical features such as indirect speech. This is a fact of language change.

Time Adverbial Clauses with {ke}

Another clause type in Dari are clauses, that act as time adverbials by indicating the time an action occurred, using an inflected time word, and/or clause introducer {ke} "when or while." Such clauses include short and long duration of time.

Examples:

/**ke** aamadom da khaana nabud/ **When** I came, he/ she was not home."
/**wakht-e** ke amrikaa bodom karima didom/ "**While** I was in America, I saw Karim."
/karima **ke** didom amrikaa bodom/ "**When** I saw Karim, I was in America."

Comparative Clauses

Clauses are also used to express comparison.

For example,
/ketaab-e dari az ketaab-e pashtow kada arzaantar-as/.
NP1+ az+ NP2+kada+Comparative Adjective

Note that, the above sentence is derived from two simple sentences: /ketaab-e dari kam qimat daara/ /ketaab-e pashtow zyaad qimat daara/, or from /ketaab-e pashtow arzaan-as amaa ketaab-e dari arzaantar/ "The Pashto book is cheap, but the Dari book is (even) cheaper."

Contrasting Clauses

There are also clauses that express contrast. Here the conjunction words used are {laaken}, {amaa}, or {waley} "but/ however." Words of contrast used at the beginning of clauses include {agarchi ke}, {baawojud-e ke}

Examples:

/ketaab khub-as **laaken** qimat-as/ "Books are good **but** they are expensive."
/karim ushyaar bacha-s **amaa** tambal/ "Karim is smart, **but** lazy."
/afghaanestaan maghbul-as **waley** amn ney-s/ "Afghanistan is beautiful **but it** is not safe."
/**baawojud-e ke** mariz bodom da kaar raftom/ "**Even though** I was sick, nonetheless I went to work."
/**agarche ke** mariz bodom da kaar raftom/ "**Although** I was sick, I went to work."

Chapter Summary

Chapter 6 is about clauses. A sentence is the largest constituent while a word is the smallest. In between there are clauses and phrases. Every language has basic or kernel sentences, whose constituents are obligatory. By definition, all the constituents of a basic sentence are obligatory. In Dari, the subject is not always obligatory and whenever it is used, its presence indicates emphasis. There are eight basic sentence types in Dari.

There are nine basic sentences in Dari. Through the process of embedding and conjoining, from the finite number of sentences (basic sentence patterns), an infinite number of sentences can be generated. In embedding, one or more basic sentences are combined to make a complex sentence. Embedding in Dari involves restrictive and nonrestrictive clauses, both of which require {ke} "that/which/ who." In conjoining, on the other hand, two or more sentences of equal weight are combined. The two most common Dari conjunctions are {wa} "and" and {yaa} "or."

Noun clauses, restrictive and nonrestrictive clauses are employed in embedding. Unlike English, there is no indirect speech in either Dari or Pashto.

Exercises

1 Indicate the sentence pattern for the following:.

    #2   /ma malem-astom/
____   /tu nanafti/
____   /ma yak daana naan kharidom/
____   /paysara bar-e karim daadi?/
____   /jamilara chi gofti/
____   /ki amrika meyra/
____   /emrowz awaa khub-as/
____   /dafatan aamad/
____   /ma dari meyfaamom/
____   /karim malem shod/

2. Are the following sentences simple (S), complex (Compl.), or compound (Comp)?

    S   /ma nameyrom/
____   /cheraa englisi nameyfaami?/
____   /ketaab-e darim kojaa-s/
____   /khaana qimat-as/
____   /ma da daftar-e karim raftom/
____   /ki karim-o-najiba did/
____   /i ketaab chand afghaani-s/
____   /ma zobaan-e pashtowra meyfaamom/
____   /i angur-e khubesh neys/
____   bora-wo-chaay kaar-as/
____   /ma arrowz dars meykhandom/

3. Analyze the following complex and compound sentences into simple ones. For example, /i khaan-ey qimat az karim-as/ can be analyzed into (1)/i khaana az karim- as/ and (2) /i khaana qimat-as/.

As another example, the deep structures of /karim-o-jamila az kaabol-astan/ are:

/karim az kaabol-as/ and /jamila az kaabol-as/

/khaan-ey lailaa dur neys/_____

/ma-wo maari naan khowrdeym/_____

/qalam-e beraadar-e laylaa peysh-e ma-s/_____

/musiqi afghaanira khosh daarom/_____

/chaakleyt-e amrikaayi khubesh-as/_____

/ma shawaana khaan-ey abdolaa meyrom/_____

/u sey daana chawki-ye kalaan kaar daara/_____

/ki goft ke awaa emrowz sard-as/_____

/aksar-e afghaanaa baaysekel-e syaara khosh daaran/_____

/aksar malemaa dars-e khub nameytan/_____

4. Translate the following into Dari. The first one is done for you.

Obama said that he would talk to Karzai can be translated as/obaamaa goft ke ma amraa-ye karzai gap meyzanom/

I need to study Dari because I'm going to Afghanistan.

_____

Why don't you leave now?_____

What is for lunch today?_____

I have to leave because we have guests tonight._____

Not all the girls speak English well._____

I don't have what you want._____

If you are hungry, the food is ready._____

Obama appointed Clinton Secretary of State.———————————

If you had gone to Mazar last month, I'd have gone along, too.

Mary says she's not coming today.———————————

PART 2

Phrase book

LANGUAGE FUNCTIONS AND TOPICS

Introduction

To communicate with Afghans and succeed, it is necessary to use Dari effectively. Using a language involves command of both language **usage** and **use**. Usage has to do with language structure (phonology, morphology, and syntax), discussed in Part 1 (Grammar). Part 2 (Phrase book) is about how to use Dari to communicate with Afghans. More specifically, the Phrase book discusses language functions and topics. Language functions involve how to ask and provide information, how to agree and disagree, how to give commands, how to apologize, how to address, and so on.

The topics include shopping, family, security, health, security, transportation, and others. The section on a particular topic begins with a dialogue providing the relevant grammatical structures. This is followed by the appropriate vocabulary which is divided into nouns, verbs, and adjectives. When relevant, each topic also includes "cultural notes." The purpose of these notes is to help the reader handle a particular topic culturally as well. For example, under the topic of Family and Kinship, the cultural notes point out that, when invited to an Afghan home, it is always good to take some candy, especially chocolate. Most Afghans do not care much about flowers. Finally, when appropriate, an Afghan proverb is also added at the end of a topic. For example, under the topic on shopping, there is a saying that /qimat bey ekmat neys arzaan beyelat/ "You get what you pay for."

Language Functions

Asking for and Providing Information

**

/**naamet chi-s**/ "What is your name?" **Informal/Familiar**
/**naamem entezaar-as**/ "My name is Entezar."

**

/**da kojaa zendagi mikoni**/ "Where do you live?**Informal/Familiar**
/**da kaabol zendagi meykonom**/ "I live in Kabul."

**

/**ezdewaaj kadi yaa mojarad-asti**/. "Are you married or single?"
Informal
/**mojarad-astom**/. "I am single."

**

/**emrowz chan shambey-s**/ "What day is today?"
/**emrowz joma-s.mardom rokhsat astan**/. "Today is Friday. People are off."

**

/**i kodaam maa-s**/ "What month is it?"
/**maay-e amal-as**/ "This is March/April."

**

/**owtal da kojaa-s**/ "Where is the hotel?"
/**nezdik-e powstakhaana-s**/ "It's near the Post ffice."

**

/**chi kaar meykoni**/ "What do you do for a living?" **Informal/
Familiar**
/**malem-astom**/ "I am a teacher."

112

**

/**chand saala-sti**/ "How old are you?" Informal/Familiar
/**bist-o-panj saala-stom**/ "I am twenty five years old."

**

/**cheqa tasil kadi**/ "How much education do you have?"
Informal/Familiar
/**faakowltara khalaas kadeym**/ "I'm a college graduate."

**

/**i chand-as**/ "How much is this?"
/**panj sad afghaani**/ "It's 500 afs."

**

/**angur kilow-ye chand as**/ "How much are grapes per kilo?"
/**kilow-ye bist afghaani**/. "Twenty afs per kilo."

**

/**paghmaan cheqa dur-as**/ "How far is Paghman?"
/**paanzda kilow metr**/ "It 15 kilometers."

**

/**nefus-e kaabol zyaad-as ya az qandaar**/ "Does Kabul have more
population or Kandahar?
/**kaabol besyaar pornefustar-as**/ "Kabul is much more populated."

**

/**awaa-ye kaabol da zemestaan chetowr-as**/ "How's the weather in
Kabul during the winter?"
/**besyaar sard-as**/. "It's very cold."
/**barf zyaad meysha**?/ "Does it snow a lot?"
/**baley, zyaad barf meysha**/. "Yes, it snows a lot."

**

/**tokhm darjan-e chand-as**/ "How much are eggs a dozen?"
/**darjan-e aftaad afghaani**/. "Seven afs."

**

/**naan daan-ey chand-as**/ "How much is a loaf of bread?"
/**asht afghaani**/. "Six afs."

**

/**ma.aashet maa-ye chand-as**/ "What is your monthly salary?
/**sey azaar afghaani**/. "Three thousand afs."

**

/**rowz-e chand kaar mikoni**/ "How much do you make a day?"
/**rowz-e sad aghaani**/. "One hundred afs per day."
/**kefaayat meykona**/ "Is it enough?"
/**ney, besyaar kam-as**/ "No, it is very little."

**

/**az kodaam qawm-asti**/ "What is your ethnicity?"
/**ma azaara-stom**/ "I'm a Hazara."

**

/**az kojaa-sti**/ "Where are you from?"
/**ma az kaabol-astom**/ "I' m from Kabul."
/**zobaane maaderit chi-s**/ "What is your mother tongue?"
/**faarsi**/ "Farsi"
/enlisi gap zada meytaani?/ "Can you speak English?"
/kam kam/ "a little"

**

/**chand beraadar daari**/ "How many brothers do you have?" **Informal**
/**beraadar nadaarom**/ "I don't have any brothers."
/**padaret kaar meykona**?/ "Does your father work?"
/**ney, taqaa.od kada**/ "No, he is retired."
/**aarusi kadi?**/ "Are you married?"
/**baley, sey awlaad daarom**/ "Yes, I have three children."

**

/**tu i aadama meshnaasi**?/ "Do you know this person?" **Informal**
/**ney, nameshnaasomesh**/ "No, I don't."

**

/**che wazifa daari**/ "What do you do for a living?" **Informal**
/**ma naldawaan-astom**/ "I'm a plumber."

**

/**da kodaam reshta tasil mikoni**/ "What are you majoring in?"
Informal

—

/resht-ey ma englisi-s/ "My major is English."
/senf-e chand-asti/ "What class are you in?"
/ma senf-e chaar-e faakowlta-astom/ "I'm a senior in college."
/ostaad-etaan ki-s/ "Who is your professor?"
/daaktar entezaar/ "Dr. Entezar."

**

/englisi gap zada meytaani?/ "Can you speak English?" **Informal**
/kam kam/ "a little"

**

/khaandan-o-naweshtana yaad daari?/ "Do you know how to read and write?" **Informal**
/baley, yaad daarom/ "Yes, I do."

**

/naan-e shaw che wakht tayaar meysha/ "When will dinner be ready?"
/taqriban yak saat baad/ "In about one hour."
/chaay-e sowb chewakht-as/ "What time is breakfast?"
/saat-e aft-e sowb/ "At seven in the morning."
**

/keryey khaana da kaabol chand-as/ "How much does it take to rent a house in
Kabul?"
/farq meykona/ "It varies/depends."
**

/id chewakht-as/ "When is the Eid?"
/kodaam id/ "Which Eid?
/id-e ramazaan/ "The Ramazan Eid."
/sey maa baad/ "Three months from now."

**

/shomaa da khaarej safar kadeyn?/ "Have you traveled abroad?" **Formal/Polite**
/ney, nakadeym/ "No, I haven't."

**

/da faamil-etan chand nafar-as/ "How many people are in your family?"
/shash nafar/ "Six people."

**

/**padaret chetowr-as**/ "How's your father?"
/**mariz-as**/ "He's sick."
/**che marizi daara**/ "What is his/her sickness?"
/**maraz-e-e qalb**/ "He's suffering from heart disease."
/**khodaa shafaa-ye aajel beteysh**/ I wish him fast recovery."

**

/**majles chand baja-s**/ "What time is the meeting?"
/**now baja**/ "It is at nine o'clock."

**

/**chaar chel chand meysha**/ "How much is 4 times 40?"
/**yaksad-o-shast**/ "It is 160."
/**aafarin**/ "Good for you."
**

/**penjaa jama nawad chand meysha**/ "How much is 50 plus 90?"
/**yaksad-o-chel**/ "It is 140."

**

/**jawaaz-e sayr daari?**/ "Do you have a driver's license?" **Informal**
/**baley, daarom**/ "Yes, I do."
**

/**kaan-etaan maghbul-as**/ "Your house beautiful."
/**tashakor**/ "Thanks"
**

/**cheraqam kampyuter daari**/ "What kind of a computer do you have?"
Informal
/**kampyutarem del-as**/ "My computer is Dell."

**

/**nambar-e teylefunet chand-as**/ "What is your telephone number?"
/**teylefun nadaarom**/ "I don't have a phone."

**

/**da baar-ey amrikaa che fekr mikoneyn**/ "What do you think about America?"
Formal
/**mardom-e amrikaara khosh daarom**/ "I like the American people."

**

/da dimukeraasi aqida daari?/ "Do you believe in democracy?"
Informal
/baley, aqida daarom/ "Yes, I do."

**

/cheraa da afghaanestaan fasaad-e edaari zyad-as/ "Why do think there is so much corruption in the Afghan government?"
/az khaater-e ke okumat-e qaanun ney-s/ "Because there is no rule of law."
/dorost-as? / "Do you agree with me?
/bikhi dorost-as/ "Absolutely."

**

/i tasmim aakheret-as?/ "Is this your final decision?
/baley/ "Yes"
/saressh baaz fekr kow/ "Think it over." **Informal**
**

/chetowr-asti/ "How are you feeling?" **Informal**
/kam-e taw daarom/ "I have a little fever."

**

/waali chetowr aadam-as/ "What do you think about the governor?"
/reshwatkhowr-as/ "He takes bribe."

**

/cheraa zeyr-e destaa shekaayat daaran/ "Why are the employees complaining?"
/az /khaater-e ke maasheshaan kam-as/ "Because they don't get paid enough."

**

/waali-ye qandaar ki-s/ "Who is the governor of Kandahar?"
/nameyfaamom/ "I don't know."

**

/afghaanaa da baar-ey amrikaa chi fekr meykonan/ "What do Afghans think about the United Sates?"
/rowz ba rowz etemaad-e khoda az dest meytan/ "Their trust is waning day by day."

**

/qomandaan-etan ki-s/ "Who is your commander?"
/gholaam qaader khaan/ "Ghulam Qadir"

**

/lotfan yak geylaas aw betey/ "Please give me a glass of water."
Polite
/ba cheshm/ "Certainly"

Greetings and Well-Wishing
/salaam/ "Hello" (Lit. peace)
/waaleykomasalaam/ "Hi" (Lit. peace be upon you)
**

/chetowr-asti/ or /chi aal daari/ "How are you?" **Informal**
/khub-astom, tashakor/ I'm fine, thank you."

**

/khodaafez/ or /khodaa aafez/ "Good-bye" (Lit. May God be your protector.)
/khodaafez/ "Good-bye"
/baamaan-e khodaa/ "Good-bye"

**

/padareta salaam bogow/ "Say hello to your father (for me)."
Informal
/ba cheshm/ "I will."

**

/shab bakhayr/ "Good night" (This expression is usually used among the educated and Westernized Afghans)
/shab bakhayr/ "Good night"

**

/rowz-e khosh baretaan meykhaayom/ "Have a good day" (Lit. I want you a happy day) **Formal**
/bar-e shomaam/ "You, too."
**

/aarusita tabrik meygom/ "Congratulations on you wedding."
Informal
/tashakor/ "Thanks"

**

/baret shafaa-ye kaamel meykhaayom/ "I wish you full recovery."
Informal
/tashakor/ "Thanks"

**

/maanda nabaashi/ "May you not (be) tired."(Used when someone comes home after work or a trip.
/zenda baashi/ "May you live."

Agreeing
/gap-e khodet dorost-as/ "You are right/ I agree with you." **Polite**
/chiz-e ke migi sayi-s/ "What you are saying is correct." **Informal**
/dorost-as/ "It is correct" or "You are right."
/maam ameto fekr meykonom/ "I feel the same way."
/gapet maaqul-as/ "What you are saying makes sense." **Informal**
/fekr-e ardu-ye maa yak chiz-as/ "You and I have the same view."
/naan kharaab bud/ "The food was bad."
/ba raasti kharaab bud/ "Indeed, it was bad."
/baley, mota.asefaana kharaab bud/ "Yes, unfortunately, it was bad."
/maam ameto fekr meykonom/ "I feel the same way."
/gap-e khodet dorost-as/ "You are right."
/nazar-e maam ami-s/ "I have the same view."
/ma amraayt mowaafeq-astom/ "I agree with you."

Disagreeing
/borrow! i dorost neys/ "Go! "This is incorrect." **Informal**
/nazar-e ma farq daara/ "My view is different."
/ma mowaafeq neystom/ "I disagree."
/gapet aw-o-daana nadaara/ "You're not making any sense."
Informal
/gap-e khodet dorost neys/ "What you saying is incorrect."
/i mokhaalef-e eslaam-as/ "This is against Islam."
/ma baayad saresh fekr bokonom/ "I will think about it."

Persuading
/aga ma eywaz-e tu baashom, i kaara nameykonom/ "If I were you, I wouldn't do it." **Informal**
/i kaar-e khub-as/ "This is the right thing to do."
/i kaar ba faaydeyt-as/ "This is to your advantage."
/ba fekr-e ma i baret khub-as/ In my view, this is good for you."
Informal

Dissuading

/aga ba jaay-et baashom, i kaara nameykonom/ "If I were you, I wouldn't do it." **Informal**

/saresh baaz fekr kow/ "Think it over." **Informal**

/i baret khub ney-s/ "This is not good for you." **Informal**

/i kaar faayda nadaara/ "This is not beneficial."

/azi kaar bogzar/ "Don't think about it." **Informal**

/gap-e mara beshnaw/ "Listen to my advice."

/bar-e yak mosolmaan i kaar khub ney-s/ "This is what Muslims should do."

Apologizing

/mazerat meykhaayom/ "I apologize." (Formal)

/mara bobakhsh/ "Forgive me." (Formal/Polite)

/baa mazerat/ "Excuse me" (Formal)

/ma ghalat kadom/ "It was my mistake." (Formal)

/khayr-as/ "It's alright." (Informal)

/parwaa nadaara/ "It's all right."

/meybakhshi/ "Excuse me." **Informal**

/gonaa-ye ma bud/ "It was my mistake/falt"

/az peysh-e ma ghalat shod/ "I made a mistake."

Ordering/ requesting

/baash!/ "Wait" (Informal)

/lotfan baasheyn/ "Wait" (Formal/Polite)

/sabr kow!/ "Be patient" (Informal)

/bofarmaayeyn/ "Please (proceed)"

/estaada show!/ "Stand up." (Informal)

/baayad bori!/ "You should go." (Informal

/byaa ke boreym/ "Let's go."

/narrow!/ "Don't go."

/baaz bogow! nafaamidom/ "/Say it again. I didn't understand."

/taal natey! / "Don't wait."

/pas byaa!/ "Come back."

/dawr bokhow/ "Turn around"

Warning

/khabardaar!/ "Watch out!"

/baakhabar!/ "Watch out!"

/pashow!/ "Move" **Informal**

/usu show!/ "Move to the side" **Informal**

/ushyaar khabardaar! Be on guard."

/ush kow!/ or /etyaat kow/ "Be careful." **Informal**

Addressing Afghans

As it has been pointed out, uneducated Afghans who make at least 90 percent of the population only have one name (See Appendix C: Afghan Names). The educated, on the other hand, usually have last names. There are formal and informal ways of addressing educated and uneducated Afghans.

If someone's full name, for example, is **Haji Sayyed Ghulam Qadir Popal**, he can be addressed as follows:

1. /aaji saayb/ **Formal**. The word "sayb" means "sir"
2. /aaji/ **Familiar/ Informal**
3. /aaji sayd gholaam qaader/ **Informal**
4. /sayd gholaam qaader khaan/ **Formal**
5. /aaghaa-ye powpal/ "Mr. Popal" **Formal**
6. /gholaam qaader aaghaa/ **Formal**. The word /aaghaa" relates to Sayyed, descendant of the Prophet Mohammad.
7. /aaghaa saayb/ **Formal**
8. /gholaam qaader jaan/ **Familiar** The word /jaan/ means "dear"
9. /gholaam qaader/ **Informal**

It is always safe to call an elderly man /**kaakaa**/ (uncle) or /**baaba jaan**/ or/**aaji**/ even he has not made the Hajj. A male person of the same age is /**byaadar**/ (brother) or /**byaadar jaan.**) An elderly woman, on the other hand, can be addressed as /**maadar**/ (mother) or /**maader jaan**/; and a female of the same age as the speaker as /**amsheya**/ (sister).

In the countryside, however, where most people are uneducated, they usually do not have last names. A person named Ghulam Mohammad should be addressed as follows:

1. /*gholaam maamad khaan*/ (Formal)
2. /*aaji saayb*/ if he has gray beard and even if has not made the Haj. (Formal)
3. /*aaji* if he has made the Hajj/(Informal)
4. /*gholaam maamad jaan*/ or /*gholaam jaan*/ if younger or the same age (Informal/Familiar)
5. /*sufi*/ or /*sufi saayb*/ if he has a black beard even if not a true mystic (The word "Sufi"/ means a mystic).

SHOPPING

1. Dialogue
**

/salaam, chetowr asti/	Hi, how are you?
/khub astom, tashakor/	I'm doing well, thanks."
/i peyraan chand-as/	How much is this shirt?
/sey sad afghaani/	300 afs
/da daalar chand meysha/	How much in dollars?
/shash daalar/	Six dollars.
/aakheresh chand-as/	What is the last price?
/aakher nadaara/	It has no last price."
/besyaar qimat-as/	It's very expensive.
/jagra nakow/	Don't bargain
/peyraan saakht-e kojaa-s/	Where was it made?"
/peyraan-e amrekaayi daari?/	Do you have American shirts?
/ney, mota.asefaana nadaarom/	No, unfortunately I don't
/peyraan-e chinaaye darom/	I have Chinese shirts.
/peraan-e aastin kowtaa meykhaayom/	I want a short-sleeve shirt.
/nomr-e yakhanem shaanzda-as/	My neck size is sixteen.
/kodaam ranga khosh daareyn/	What color do you like?
/safeyd/	White.
/bist daalarira polesya daari?/	Do you have change for $20?
/ney, nadaarom. baaqisha afghaani betom?/	No, I don't. Can I give the rest in afs?
/baley, farq nameykona/.	Yes. It is doesn't make any difference.

—

122

**

/angur chandi-s/ How much are grapes?
/kilow-ye penjaa/ Fifty afs per kilo.
/sherin-as?/ Are they sweet?
/baley, besyaar sherin-as/ Yes, they are very sweet."
/raas migi?/ Really?
/tarbuz daan-ey chand-as/ How much watermelons?

2. Nouns.

/lebaas/ "clothing"

/obubaat/ "grains"

/dokhaneyaat/ "tobacco"

/meywajaat/ "fruits"

/nektaayi/ "necktie"

/kinow/ "tangerine"

/desmaal/ "handkerchief"

/qaalincha/ "a small rug "

/but/ "shoe"

/saabun/ "soap"

/raadeyow/ "radio"

/kaset / "cassette"

/kamputar/ "computer"

/baalapowsh/ "overcoat"

/chatri/ "umbrella"

/atreyat/ "perfumes"

/araadajaat/ "vehicles"

/mokhadaraat/ "narcotics"

/joraab/ "socks"

/korti/ "coat"

/qaalin/ "rug"

/kolaa/ "hat, cap"

/destaar/ "turban"

/shampoo/ "shampoo"

/kaamra/ "camera"

/talwezyun/ "television"

/cidi / "CD"

/fita/ "tape"

/derishi/ "suit"

3. Verbs

/kharidan/ "to buy"

/jagra kadan/ chana zadan/ "to bargain"

/sawdaa kharidan/ "to shop"

/khowrdan/ "to eat"

/aawordan/ "to bring"

/forowkhtan/ "to sell"

/sawdaa kadan/ "to make a sale"

/bay kadan/ "to ask price"

/pas daadan/ "to return"

/pokhta kadan/ "to cook"

4. Adjectives

/khub/ "good"

/kharaab/ "bad"

/arzaan/ "cheap"	/qimat/ "expensive"
/kalaan/ "big/large"	/khord/ "small"
/daraaz/ "long"	/kowtaa/ "short"
/asl/ "real"	/badal/ "fake"
/zyaad/ "more"	/kam/ "little/less"
/sherin/ "sweet"	/talkh/ "bitter"
/taaza/ "fresh"	/khoshk/ "dry"
/besyaar/ "a lot/plenty"	/kam/ "less"
/khaales/ "pure"	/makhlut/naakhaales/ "mixed/impure"
/paak/ "clean"	/chatal/kasif/naapaak/ "dirty, unclean"
/chaalaak/ "shrewd"	/saada/ "naive/plain"
/mofid/ "useful/nutritious"	/mozer/ "useless/unhealthy"
/ushyaar/ "smart"	/lawda/beyaql/ "stupid"

5. Cultural Notes

- For more information and explanation on the cultural notes in this book, please refer to *Afghanistan 101: Understanding Afghan Culture* (2008).
- In Afghanistan, prices are not usually fixed. Therefore, it's better to bargain when shopping or negotiating a deal.

/qatra qatra daryaa meysha/
"A river is made drop by drop."
Afghan Proverb

FRUITS AND VEGETABLES

1. Dialogue

/angur kilow-ye chand-s/	"How much are grapes per kilo?"
/bist afghaani/	"Twenty afs."
/qimat-as./ arzaan nameysha?/	"They are expensive. How about a bit cheaper?"
/qimat beyekmat neys arzaan beyelat/	"You get what you pay for."(an Afghan proverb).
/char kilow towl kow/	"Give me four kilos."
/ba cheshm/	"Glad to."

2. Nouns

/angur/ "grapes"

/seyb/ "apple"

/tarbuz/ "watermelon"

/shaftaalu/ "peach"

/geylaas/ "cherry"

/maalta/ "orange"

/baadaam/ "almond"

/chaarmaghz/ "walnut"

/tarkaari/ "vegetables"

/paalak/ "spinach"

/moli/ "white or red turnip"

/kachaalu/ "potato"

/pyaaz/ "onion"

/gandana/ "leeks"

/naak/ "pears"

/anaar/ "pomegranate"

/kharbuza/ "melon"

/zardaalu/ "apricot"

/naarenj/ "sour orange"

/keshmesh/ "raisins"

/pesta/ "pistachios"

/keyla/ "banana"

/kaawu/ "lettuce"

/zardak/ "carrot"

/shalgham/ "turnip"

/nowshpyaaz/ "green onion"

/sir/ "garlic"

/baadrang/ "cucumber"

/khalta/ "bag"

/satl/ "bucket"

/tarkaari forowsh/ "green grosser"

/sandoq/ "box"

/jwaal/ "sack"

/meywa forowsh/ "fruit seller"

3. Verbs

/towl kadan/ "to weigh"

/khalta kadan/ "bagging"

/zyad kadan/ "to increase/add"

/jowr aamadan/ "to make a deal"

/andaakhtan/ "to pour"

/kam kadan/ "to lessen"

/kamdaadan/ "to pay less"

4. Adjectives

/taaza/ "fresh"

/talkh/ "bitter"

/awdaar/ "juicey"

/baasi/ "old/leftover"

/kalaan/ "large/big"

/arzaan/ "cheap"

/ganda/ "rotten"

/sobok/ "light"

/narm/ "soft"

/arzaanforowsh/ "one who sells cheap"

/khoshk/ "dry"

/sherin/ "sweet"

/mazadaar/ "tasty"

/kowna/ "old"

/khord/ "small"

/qimat/ "expensive/pricy"

/kharaab/ "bad"

/gerang/ "heavy"

/sakht/ "hard"

/qimatforowsh/ "one who overcharges"

/tond/ "spicey hot"

/showr/ "salty"

/lezat-e donyaa zan-o dandaan bowad/
"The two pleasures of life are women and teeth."
Afghan Proverb

Travel and Transportation

1. Dialogue

/**i sarweys kojaa meyra**/ "Where does this bus go?"
/**beymaaru meyra**/ "It goes to Bemaroo."
**

/**taa kotey sangi chand meybari**/ "How much is it to Kotay Sangi?"
/**do sad afghaani**/ "Two hundred afs."
/**kam nameysh**?/ "How about less than that?"
/**nakhayr**/ "No."
**

/**keraayet chand shod**/ "How much is/was the fare?"
**

/**lowgar cheqa dur-as**/ "How far is Logar?"
/**yak saat raa-s**/ "It's about an hour's drive."

2. Nouns

/mowtar/ "car"   /baaysekel/ "bicycle"
/taksi/ "taxi"   /tayaara/ "aircraft"
/mosaafer/ "passenger/traveler"   /teket/ "ticket"
/yak tarafa/ "one way"   /do tarafa/ "round trip/two ways"
/sarweys/ "bus"   /tayr/ "tire"
/tub/ "tube"   /engen/maashin/ "engine, machine"
/teyl/ "gas"   /moblaayl/ "oil"

/esteyshan-e teyl/ "gas station"
/rasturaan/ "restaurant"
/keraa/ "fare/rent"
/raas/ "right"
/robruy/ "straight"
/esteyshan/ "station"
/esteyshan-e polis/ "police station"
/laari/ "truck"
/khar/ "donkey"
/mowtarskel/ "motorbike"
/karaachi/ "cart"
/shotor/ "camel"
/aqol obur/ "road toll"
/maydaan-e tayaara/ "airport"
/talaashi/ "search"
/paaspowrt/ "passport"
/tank-e teyl/ "gas station"
/teyl-e khaak/ "kerosene"
/pyaada/ "on foot"
/khaw/ "sleep"

/owtal/ "hotel/restaurant"
/khowraak/ "diet/food/order"
/eshtereng/ "steering wheel"
/chap/ "left"
/baghal/ "side/by"
/saakht/ "made"
/karaachi/ "cart"
/reyl/ "train"
/asp/ "horse"
/gaadi/ "buggy, horse-ridden cart"
/qaater/ "mule"
/paatak/ "roadblock"
/teket forush/ "Ticketing office"
/gomrok/ "customs"
/maasul/ "tax/duty"
/wiza/ "visa"
/modireyat-e taraafik/ "traffic office"
/mowtarwan/ "driver"
/swaari/ "passenger"
/beydaar/ "awake"

3. Verbs

/tarmim kadan /jowr kadan/ "to fix/repair"
/swaari bowrdan/ "to carry passengers"
/kam kadan/ "lessening/reducing"
/baala/swaar shodan/ "to ride or hopping in"
/berek zadan/ "to apply the brake"
/panchar shodan/ "to have a flat"
/paak kadan/ "to clean"
/jaaru kadan/ "to sweep"
/khaali kadan/ "to empty/pour"
/rawaan kadan/ "to send"

/safar kadan/ "to travel"
/jagra kadan/ "to bargain"
/estaad shodan/ tawqof kadan/ "to stop"
/paayaan shodan/ "to get off"
/dawr khowrdan/ "to turn"
/shoshtan/ "to wash"
/forowkhtan/ "to sell"
/baad kadan/ "to pump"
/por kadan/ "to fill"
/aawordan/ "to bring"

/dawaandan/ "to make someone/ something run"

/kharidan/ "to buy"

/farmaayesh daadan/ "ordering"

/teyz raftan/ "speeding"

/tawaqof kadan/ "to stop"

/maatel shodan/ "to wait/delay"

4. Adjectives

/nezdik/	"near"	/dur/	"far"
/arzaan/	"cheap"	/qimat/	"expensive"
/teyz/	"fast/sharp"	/aastaa/	"slow"
/khord/	"small"	/teyz/	"fast"
/aasataa/	"slow"	/beyetyaat/	"careless"

SECURITY

1. Dialogue

/chi wazifa daari/ "What's your job/What do you do for a living?"
/mansabdaar-astom/ "I'm a (military officer)."
/rotbeyt chi-s/ "What's your rank?"
/ma dagarwaal-astom/ "I'm a colonel."
/kaaret da kojaa-s/ "Where do you work?"
/da wezaarat-e defaa/ "At the Ministry of Defense."

2. Nouns

/polis/ "police"

/askari/ "military"

/defaa/ "defense"

/mansabdaar/saaybmansab/ "officer"

/ordu/ "army"

/gaard/maafez/ "guard"

/ferqa/ "corps"

./tofang/ "gun"

/towp/ "cannon"

/alowkaaptar/ "helicopter"

/but/ "boots"

/jabakhaana/ "ammunition"

/sawaal/ "question'

/amr/ "order, command"

/askar/ "soldier"

/wezaarat/ "ministry"

/amneyat/ "security"

/genraal/ "general"

/meli/ "national"

/qomandaan/ "commandant"

/kandak/ "battalion"

/maashindaar/ "machine gun"

/marmi/ "bullets, ammunition"

/derishi askari / "military uniform"

/peyraan/ "shirt"

/layleya/qaaghowsh / "dormitory"

/jawaab/ "answer"

/ta.aamkhaana/ "dining room"

/talimgaa/ "drill area"

/salaa/ "weapon"

/pyaada/ "infantry"

/estekhbaaraat/ "intelligence"

/qaatel/ "murderer"

/kisabor/ "pickpocket"

/akhtaar/ "warning"

/majles/ "meeting"

/reshwat/ "bribe"

/fesaad/ "corruption"

/kaard/ "kitchen knife"

/ghar-e nezaami/ "civilian"

/doshman/ "enemy"

/bam/ "bomb"

/bam-e desti/ "hand grenade"

/maamur/ "employee"

/bandi/ "prisoner"

/qaazi/ "judge"

/mokhber/ "spy"

/jang /maareba/ "war/fight"

/amneyat-e meli/ "national security"

/tupchi/ "artillery"

/doz/ "thief"

/jorm/ "crime"

/taqaawod/ "retirement"

/tasil/ "education/schooling"

/jaasus/ "spy"

/waaseta/ "connection"

/chaaqu/ "pocket knife"

/maslak/ "occupation/specialty"

/nezaami/ "military"

/dowst/ "friend"

/amla/ "attack"

/barcha/ "bayonet"

/aamer/ "boss"

/bandikhaana/ "jail"

/maakama/ "court of law"

3. Verbs

/payra kadan/ "to patrol/guard"

/tarfi kadan/ "being promoted"

/dars daadan/ "to teach"

/emeteyaan daadan/ "to take a test/ exam"

/sawaal kadan/ "to ask"

/etaaat kadan/ "to obey"

/doshmani kadan/ "to engage in animosity"

/tabdil kadan/ "to transfer someone"

/bartaraf kadan/ "to fire someone"

/paydaa kadan, paalidan/ "to find, search"

/naakaam shodan/ "to fail" /

/faaregh shodan/ "to graduate"

/jazaa daadan/ "to punish"

/maaquf shodan/ "to be fired"

/dars khaandan/ "to study"

/emteyaan gereftan/ "to give a test"

/jawaab daadan/ "to answer"

/fayr kadan/ "to fire a weapon"

/neshaan gereftan/ "to take an aim"

/moqarar kadan/ "to appoint"

/dozi kadan/ "to steal"

/akhtaar daadan/ "to warn"

/kaamyaab shodan/ "to pass/ succeed"

4. Adjectives

/moti/ "obedient" /baaghi/ "rebel"
/beyparwaa/ "careless/sloppy" /tambal/ "lazy"
/zaamatkash/ "studious" /sharif/ "noble"
/beysharaf/ "ignoble" /badakhlaaq/ "immoral"
/ba.aakhlaaq/ "moral" /faased/ "corrupt"
/beysharaf/ "ignoble" /tambal/ "lazy"

/aftaw da do angosht pot nameysha/
The sun cannot be covered with two fingers.
Afghan Proverb

FAMILY AND RELATIONS

1. Dialogue

/da khaan-ey maa khosh aamadi/ "Welcome to our house."
/khosh baashi/ "Thank you," (lit. You be happy.)
/faamil-e shomaa khub-as?/ "Are your family members in good health?"
/tashakor, khub-astan/ "They are fine. Thank you."

2. Nouns

/padar/ "father"

/maadar/ "mother"

/beraadar/ byaadar/ "brother"

/khwaar/ or/amsheyra/ "sister"

/kaakaa/ "paternal uncle"

/maamaa/ "maternal uncle"

/ama/ "paternal aunt"

/khaala/ "maternal aunt"

/daamaat/ "son-in-law"

/khosor/ "father-in-law"

/khoshu/ "mother-in-law"

/keyaashna/ "sister-in-law"

/ambaaq/ "cowife"

/aarows/ or /sonow/ "daughter-in-law"

/khosurbora/ "brother-in-law"

/kheyshaa/" relative"

/kosorbora/ "son-in-law"

/padarkalaan/ "grandfather"

/khosorkheyl/ "in-laws"

/maamaa khosor/ "wife's maternal uncle"

/kaakaa khosor/ "wife's paternal uncle"

/naamzaad/ "fiancé"

/maadarkalaan/ "grandmother"

/kheysha/ "relative"

/meymaankhaana/ "guestroom"

/otaaq-e khaw/ "bedroom"

/chaprkat/ "bed"

/kawch/ "couch/sofa"

/chawki/ "table"

/meyz/ "table"

/baalesht/ "pillow"

/towshak/ "mattress"

/ruyjaayi/ "sheet"

/aashpazkhaana/ "kitchen"

/group/ "lightbulb"

/destarkhaan/ "tablecloth"

/showla/ "a rice dish"

/kechriqorut/ "rice dish with curd"

/qowrma/ "stew"

/ferni/ "pudding"

/chaay/ "tea"

/chalaw/ "white cooked rice"

/beshqaab/ "plate"

/kaasa/ "bowl"

/panja/ "fork"

/deyg/ "pot"

/morch/ "peper"

/sherni khuri/ "engagement party"

/meymaan/ "guest"

/chaa-ye sowb/ "breakfast"

/naan-e shaw/ "dinner"

/noql/ "candy, usually sugar coated almonds"

/saalan/ "side dish"

/rowghan/ "shortening"

/khowraak/ "order/ meal/feed"

/morch/ "pepper"

/parda/ "curtain"

/saalun/ "living room"

/cheraagh/ "light"

/palaw/ "brown cooked rice"

/chalaw/ "white cooked rice"

/qaabeli/ "rice dish with carrots and raisins"

/shirberenj/ "rice cooked with milk and sugar"

/dowgh/ "yogurt"

/bura/ "sugar"

/showla/ "sticky rice dish"

/ghuri/ "platter"

/qaashoq/ "spoon"

/kard/ "knife"

/naan/ "Afghan bread"

/namak/ "salt"

/aarusi/ "wedding"

/ambaaq/ "cowife"

/naan-e chasht/ "lunch"

/chaay/ "tea"

/meywa/ "fruit"

/sharbat/ "juice"

/bakhshesh/ "tip"

/namak/ "salt"

/masaala/ "spice"

3. Verbs

/aarusi kadan/ "to get married"

/lat kadan/ "to beat someone"

/khowrdan/ "to eat/drink"

/jowrporsaani kadan/ "to greet"

/paak kadan/ "to clean"

/salaam daadan/ "to say hello"

/naamzad shodan/ "to get engaged"

/meymaan kadan/ "to invite"

/khaw kadan/ "to sleep"

/tabdil kadan/ "to change"

/jaaru kadan/ "to sweep"

/shoshtan/ "to wash"

4. Adjectives

/paak/ "clean"	/chatal/ "dirty"
/mazadaar/ "tasty"	/showr/ "salty"
/kalaan/ "big"	/khord/ "small"
/dur/ "far"	/nezdik/ "near"
/besyaar/ "plenty"	/kam/ "less"
/sherin/ "sweet"	/talkh/ "bitter"
/tond/ "hot, spicy"	/daagh/ "hot, temp."
/sard/ "cold"	/garm/ "warm/fresh"
/awgin/ "weak tea"	/tira/ "strong (tea, soup)"
/charb/ "greasy"	/khaam/ "raw/undercooked"
/baasi/ "leftover"	/kowna/ "old"

5. Cultural Notes

- It is always good to bring a gift usually chocolate or candy when invited to an Afghan home.
- Don't ask anything about the female members of an Afghan family. Talk about the male members, income, property, and others.
- Be prepared to hear questions that are personal in the American culture: salary, marital status, age, and, other personal matters. It is better to change the subject, unless you want to talk about those issues.
- Avoid discussing religion.

/Az sad beygaana kada yak az khod beytar-as/
One relative is better than a hundred strangers.
Afghan Proverb

EDUCATION

1. Dialogue

/da kodaam powantun-asti/	"Which university are you attending?" **Informal**
/powantun-e kaabol/	"Kabul University."
/senf-e chand-asti/	"Which year?"
/da senf-e awal-astom/.	"I'm a freshman."
/da kodaam reshta/	"In what field?"
/ma saayns meykhaanom/	"I'm studying science."

2. Nouns

/shaagerd/ "elementary/high school student"

/malem/ "elementary/high school teacher"

/mazmun/ "subject"

/kowrs/ "course"

/emteyaan/ "test/exam/ quiz"

/eskaalarshep/ "scholarship"

/maasteri/ maafawq-e leysaans/ "master"

/leysaans/ "under graduate degree"

/ejtemaayaat/ "social sciences"

/taarikh/ "history"

/byaaluzhi/ "biology"

/adabeyaat/ "literature"

/mo.asel/ "college student"

/ostaad/ "college professor"

/reshta/ "field, major"

/tasil/ "study, schooling"

/faareghotasil/ "graduate"

/shaadatnaama/ "diploma"

/daaktari/ "doctorate"

/teb/ "medicine"

/olum-e tabi.i/ "natural sciences"

/joghraafeya/ "geography"

/kimyaa/ "chemistry"

/zobaan/ "language"

/sheyr/ "poetry"

/maqaala/ "article"

/kaaghaz/ "paper"

/qalam/ "pen"

/ketaab/ "book"

/ketaabcha/ "notebook"

/dars/ "lesson/study"

/lekchar/ "lecture"

/kaar-e khaanagi/ "homework"

/faakowlta/ or /powanzay "college, faculty"

/bakalowreyaa/ "a high school diploma"

/maastari/ "masters"

/daaktari/ "doctorate"

/talimaat/ "education"

/ebtedaayi/ "elementary"

/motawaseta/ "middle school"

/saanawi/ "secondary"

/madrasa/ "religious school"

/kaaghaz/ "paper"

/ketaab/ "book"

/fis/ "tuition"

/eskaalarship/ "scholarship"

3. Verbs

/nowt gereftan/ "to take notes"

/tasil kadan/ "to study"

/tashri daadan/ "to explain"

/jowaab daadan/ "to answer/respond"

/ghalat kadan/ "to make a mistake"

/sayi kadan/ "to correct/fix"

/shaamel shodan/ "to enroll/enlist"

/faaregh shodan/ "to graduate"

/shaadatnaama/ "diploma"

/dars daadan/ "to teach"

/lekchar daadan/ "to lecture"

/sawaal kadan/ "to ask"

4. Adjectives

/laayeq/ "competent, capable"

/naalaayeq/ "incompetent, incapable"

/beysewaad/ "non-literate"

/baasewaad/ "literate"

/talimyaafta/ "educated"

/beytalim/ "uneducated"

/zaki/ "intelligent, smart"

/zaamatkash/ "hard working"

5. Cultural Notes

In teaching Afghans, it's crucial to establish authority the very first day of class. This can be achieved if you are serious, prepared, and competent in the subject, and if you are fair and firm. Afghans respect authority of the person rather than authority of the rule or of the position.

Health and Hygiene

1. Dialogue

**

/kojaa miri/ "Where are you going?" **Informal**
/peysh-e daaktar meyrom/ "I'm going to the doctor."
/chi marizi daari/ "What sickness do you have?"
/poshtem dard meykona/ "I have a back ache."

2. Nouns

/mariz/ "patient"

/dawaa/ "medicine"

/dawaakhaana/ "pharmacy"

/nars/ "nurse"

/shafaakhaana/ "hospital"

/guli/ "tablets"

/fis/ "fee"

/tadaawi/ "treatment"

/taw/ "fever"

/khun/ "blood"

/dest/ "hand"

/paay/ "foot"

/bini/ "nose"

/dandaan/ "tooth"

/gorda/ "kidney"

/marizi/ "sickness"

/shafaa/ "recovery"

/maraz/ "disease"

/qaabela/ "midwife"

/kelenik/ "clinic"

/kapsowl/ "capsule"

/se.at/ "health"

/solfa/ "coughing"

/feshaar/ "pressure"

/shakar/ "sugar"

/shaana/ "shoulder"

/cheshm/ "eye"

/daan/ "mouth"

/del, qalb/ "heart"

/jegar/ "liver"

/sar/ "head"

/angosht /kelk/ panja/ "finger, toe"

/mekrowb/ "microbe/germs"

/noskha/ "prescription"

/amaleyaat/ "operation"

/jaraayi/ "surgery"

/edraar/ "urine"

/reyzesh/ "cold"

/bestari/ "hospitalized"

/beyush/ "unconscious"

/muy/ "hair"

/sardardi/ "headache"

/peych/ "dysentery"

/bors/ "brush"

/kerim-e dandaan/ "toothpaste"

/towfa/ "present/gift"

/sartabib/ "hospital director"

/ambowlaans/ "ambulance"

/warzesh/ "exercise"

/kamowd/ "toilet"

/zaanu/ "knee"

/kamar/ "waist"

/shosh/ "lungs"

/zowf/ "faint"

/jaraa/ "surgeon"

/peychkaari/ "injection"

/mawaad-e ghaayeta/ "stool"

/esteraa.at/ "rest"

/leng/ "legs"

/bey.es/ "numb"

/powst/jeld/ "skin"

/esaal/ "diarrhea"

/qabz/ "constipation"

/kerim/ "cream"

/malam/ "ointment"

/powdar/ "powder"

/maawen/ "assistant"

/bestar/ "bed"

/tashnaab/ "restroom"

/noskha/ "prescription"

3. Verbs

/mo.aayena kadan/ "to examine/check"

/jelawgiri kadan/ "to prevent"

/esteraaat kadan/ "to rest"

/mowrdan/ "to die"

/jowr shodan/ "to recover"

/bestari shodan/ "to hospitalize"

/koshtan/ "to kill"

/zakhmi kadan/ "to injure someone"

/gharghara kadan/ "to gargle/hang"

/tadaawi kadan/ "to treat"

/reyzesh kadan/ "to catch a cold"

/pareyz kadan/ "to avoid eating/drinking certain food and drinks"

/zowf kadan/ "to faint"

/mariz shodan/ "to become sick"

/koshta shodan/ "to get killed"

/awgaar kadan/ "to hurt"

/beyush kadan/ "to make unconscious"

/bors kadan/ "to brush"

4. Adjectives

/zaif/ "weak"

/awgaar/ "hurt"

/aajel/ "urgent/emergency"

/qawi/ "strong"

/zakhmi/ "injured"

/se.atmand/ "healthy"

Religion and Worship

1. Dialogue

/ramazaan chewakht-as/ "When is the fasting month?"
/yak maa baad/ "A month from now."
/chand rowz dawaam meykona/ "How long does it last?"
/si rowz/ "Thirty days."

2. Nouns

/namaaz/ "praying"

/din/ "religion"

/khodaa/ "God"

/soni/ "Sunni"

/mazab/ "sect"

/zakaat/ "almsgiving"

/aaji/ "one has done Hajj"

/zyaarat/ "shrine"

/molaa/ "cleric"

/kaafer/ "infidel"

/isawi/ "Christian"

/isaa payghombar/ "Jesus the Prophet"

/sawaab/ "spiritual reward"

/aq/ "legitimate/right"

/alaal/ "permitted according to Islam"

/qaari/ "reciter (of the Koran)"

/rowza/ "fasting"

/aqida/ "faith"

/payghombar/ "Prophet"

/shuya/ "Shiite"

/mosolmaan/ "Muslim"

/aj/ "pilgrimage"

/do.aa/ "pray"

/maajet/masjed/ "mosque"

/qaazi/ "judge"

/je.aad/ "holy war"

/yawudi/ "Jew"

/shayid/ "martyr"

/gonaa/ "sin"

/naa.aq/ "illegitimate"

/araam/ "prohibited in Islam"

/janat/ "Paradise"

/dowzaq/ "Hell"

/jaaynamaaz/ "a prayer rug"

/jenaaza/ "funeral"

/aakherat/ "Judgment Day"

/tazbey/ "beads"

3. Verbs

/namaaz khaandan/ "to pray"

/aj raftan/ "to make the pilgrimage to Mecca"

/zyaarat kadan/ "to visit (a shrine)"

/rowza gereftan/ "to fast"

/aaji shodan/ "to become a Haji"

4. Adjectives

/baakhodaa/ "religious"

/raastgowy/ "honest"

/aadel/ "just"

/monaafeq/ "hypocritical"

/motaqi/ "pious"

/beykhodaa/ "irreligious"

/dorowghgowy/ "dishonest"

/zaalem/ "cruel/ a cruel person"

/dindaar/ "religious"

/mazabi/ "religious"

5. Cultural Notes

- As it has been pointed out, it is best to avoid any discussion on religion, and politics with Afghans. If you are Jewish, never mention it.
- Allow your Afghan subordinates to take time to pray or attend funerals. However, make sure they are truthful.
- If you are a female, dress conservatively. Wear a scarf, a skirt, and a long-sleeve shirt.

Weather and Climate

1. Dialogue

**

/**awaa emrowz chetowr-as**/ "How's the weather today?"
/**emrowz besyaar garm-as**/ "It's very hot today."
/**chand daraja-s**/ "How hot?"
**

/**markaz garmi daareyn?**/ "Do you have central heating?"
/**nakhayr az baadpaka estefaada meykoneym**/ "No. We use fans."
/**baaz-e mardom shawaana da bam khaw meyshan**/ "Some people sleep on the roof at night."

2. Nouns

/garmi/ "heat"	/sardi/ "cold"
/awaa/ "weather/air"	/aab-o-awaa/ "climate"
/baar/ "Spring"	/taabestaan/ "summer"
/khazaan/ or /tirmaa/ "fall"	/zemestaan/ "winter"
/baaraan/ "rain"	/barf/ "snow"
/jaala/ "hail"	/yakh/ "ice/cold"
/mowtadel/ "moderate"	/gel/ or/laay "mud"
/seyl/ "flood"	/baam/ "roof"
/daryaa/ "river"	/chakak/ "leaking"
/tufaan/ "storm"	/khoshksaali/ "drought"
/bar/ "sea"	/jowy/ "creak"
/zoghaal/ "charcoal"	/chowb/ "wood"

/teyl-e khaak/ "kerosene "

/sandali/ "table covered with quilt"

/aatesh/ "fire"

/chowb/ "wood"

/kampal/ "blanket"

/pashm/ "wool"

/balut/ "oak"

/fasl/ "season"

/barq/ "power/electricity"

/fasl/ "season"

/markaz garmi/ "central heating"

/gorup/ "light bulb"

/aw/ "water"

/bokhaari/ "stove"

/lyaaf/ "quilt"

/khaakestar/ "ashes"

/zoghaal/ "charcoal"

/destkash/ "gloves"

/pashmi/ "woolen"

/raashpeyl/ "shovel"

/barfkowch/ "avalanche"

/bokhaar/ "steam"

/gaz/ "gas"

/sham/ "candle"

/baadpaka/ "fan"

3. Verbs

/garm kadan/ "to heat"

/aatesh kadan/ "to build a fire"

/gol kadan/ "to extinguish"

/garmi kadan/ "to get hot"

/chaalaan kadan/ "to start"

/sard kadan/ "to cool"

/dar daadan/ "to start a fire"

/rowshan kadan/ "to turn on fire/lights"

/paka kadan/ "to fan"

/aw aawordan/ "to fetch water"

4. Adjectives

/garm/ "hot/warm"

/mowtadel/ "moderate"

/taaqatfarsaa/ "unbearable"

/sard/ "cold"

/shadid/ "harsh/ severe"

/khoshaayand/ "pleasant"

**/az palaw kada alaw beytar-as/
Fire/heat is better than the Palaw dish.
(Afghan proverb)**

Government and Politics

1. Dialogue

/da afghaanestaan chand ezb-as/ "How many political parties are there in Afghanistan?
/nameyfaamom. shayad panj yaa shash ezb baasha/ "I don't know. There might be five or six political parties."
/kodaamesh besyaar fa.aal-as/ "Which one is more active?"
/yaki dotaaysh/ "A couple of them."

2. Nouns

/okumat/ "government"

/rayis-e dawlat/ "head of state"

/rays-e jamur/ "president"

/sadr-e aazam/ "prime minister"

/meshraanow jerga/ sanaa "the senate"

/khaareja/ "foreign affairs"

/maaleya/ "finance"

/defaa/ "defense"

/saradaat/ "borders"

/pelaan/ "plan"

/estara maakama/ "the supreme court"

/maakama/ "court"

/sefaarat/ "embassy"

/parlomaan/ "parliament"

/kaabina/ "cabinet"

/maawen-e rayis-e jamur/ "vice president"

/wolosi jerga/ "the house of representative"

/wazir/ "minister"

/daakhela/ "interior"

/tojaarat/ "commerce"

/ma.aaref/ "education"

/farang/ "culture"

/adleya/ "justice"

/qaazi/ "judge"

/safir/ "ambassador"

/seyaasat/ "politics"

/seyaasatmadaar/ "politician"

/khaareji/ "foreigner"

/qow-ey ejraayiya/ "the executive branch"

/qow-ey moqanena/ "the legislative branch"

/qow-ey qazaaya/ "the judiciary branch"

/sanaatowr/ "senator"

/ozw-e wolosi jerga/ "member of the house"

/moin/ "deputy minster"

/waali/ "governor"

/aakem/ "sub-governor"

/kaarmand/ "employee"

/mozaa.era/ "demonstration"

/reshwat/ "bribe"

/fesaad/ "corruption"

/ekhtelaas/ "embezzlement"

/taqalob/ "cheating/ fraud"

/entekhaabaat/ "elections"

/kheyaanat/ "treason"

/khaayen/ "traitor"

/jaasus/ "spy"

/destneshaanda/ "puppe**t**"

/nowkar/ "servant"

/baadaar/ "boss/ master"

/qowaa-ye naatow/ "NATO Forces"

/qowaa-ye eytelaaf/ "coalition forces"

3. Verbs

/taqalob kadan/ "to cheat/defraud"

/reshwat khowrdan/ "to take bribes"

/okumat kadan/ "to govern/ "to govern"

/edaara kadan/ "to manage"

/kheyaanat kadan/ "to commit treason"

/fereyb daadan/ "to fool/cheat"

/reshwat daadan/ "to bribe"

/kheysh khuri kadan/ "to engage in nepotism"

/mo.aamela kadan/ "to make a deal/ compromise"

/moqarar kadan/ "to appoint"

/seyaasat kadan/ "to play politics"

/jeyb por kadan/ "to fill one's pockets"

/jaasusi kadan/ "to spy"

/mokhberi kadan/ "to spy"

4. Adjectives

/beykefaayat/ "incompetent"

/naalaayeq/ "unqualified"

/beywejdaan/ "a person of no conscience"

/chaapalus/ "an apple polisher"

/charb zobaan/ "good at playing with words"

/watandowst/ "patriotic"

/saadeq/ "honest"

/watan forowsh/ "traitor"

5. Cultural Notes

1. In Afghan society during the last thirty years, it has been the government of the ruler(s), by the ruler(s), and for the ruler(s) instead of government of the people, for the people, and by the people. There, it is the rule of ruler rather than the rule of law.
2. Social power is coercive. One comes to power by force and is ousted by force. The end justifies the means. Force is the only language Afghans understand.
3. The Afghan rally behind family, ethnicity, sect, region, and ideology rather than the constitution, the flag, or the national anthem. Thus national interests are secondary.

BIBLIOGRAPHY

The sources consulted for this study

Bauer, Laurie. *English Word-formation*, Cambridge: Cambridge University Press, 1983.

Entezar, Ehsan. *Farsi (Afghan Persian) Reference Manual* The School for International Training, Putney, Vermont, USA, 1964.

_____*Intermediate Dari* U.S. Peace Corps, Kabul Afghanistan 1965.

_____*Dari* The University of Texas at Austin, Austin, Texas, USA. 1966.

_____*Afghanistan 101: Understanding Afghan Culture*, USA. Xlibris Corporation, 2008

Huddleston, Rodney, *English Grammar: an* outline, Cambridge: Cambridge University Press, 1988

Ladefoged, Peter. *A Course in Phonetics*. New York: Harcourt Brace Jovanovich, Inc. 1982.

Leech, Geoffrey and Svartvik, Jan, *A Communicative Grammar of English*. Singapore: Kyodo-Shing Loong Printing Industries Ltd 1975

Lewis, Bernard and Churchill, Buntzie, *Islam: The Religion And the People*: Pearson Education Inc.2009

Simpson, J.M.Y. *A First Course in Linguistics*, Edinburgh University Press. 1981

Fromkin, Victoria and Rodman, Robert. *An Introduction to Language*, New York:CBS College Publishing 1983.

Appendix A

Days and Months

Days of the Week

/**shambey**/ "Saturday"   /**yak shambey**/ "Sunday"

/**do shambey**/ "Monday"   /**sey shambey**/ "Tuesday"

/**chaar shambey**/ "Wednesday"   /**panj shambey**/ "Thursday"

/**joma**/ "Friday"

Saturday is like Monday in the west for people until Thursday afternoon, and Friday is off.

Months of the Year

/**amal**/ (March 21)   /**sawr**/

/**jawzaa**/   /**sarataan**/

/**asad**/   /**sombola**/

/**mizaan**/   /**aqrab**/

/**qaws**/   /**jadi**/

/**dalw**/   /**ut**/

New Year on the first /amal/ is corresponding to 31 March in the Gregorian calendar.

Appendix B

Numerals

I. Cardinal Numbers

/**yak**/ "one"

/**du**/ "two"

/**sey**/ "three"

/**chaar**/ "four"

/**panj**/ "five"

/**shash**/ "six"

/**aft**/ "seven"

/**asht**/ "eight"

/**now**/ "nine"

/**da**/ "ten"

/**yaazda**/ "eleven"

/**dwaazda**/ "twelve"

/**seyzda**/ "thirteen"

/**chaarda**/ "fourteen"

/**paanzda**/ "fifteen"

/**shaanzda**/ "sixteen"

/**abda**/ "seventeen"

/**azhda**/ "eighteen"

/**nozda**/ "nineteen"

/**bist**/ "twenty"

/**bist-o-yak**/ "twenty-one"

/**si**/ "thirty"

/**si-wo-yak**/ "thirty-one"

/**chel**/ "forty"

/**chel-o-yak**/ "forty-one"

/**penjaa**/ "fifty"

/**penjaa-wo-yak**/ "fifty-one"

/**shast**/ "sixty"

/**shast-o-yak**/ "sixty one"

/**aftaad**/ "seventy"

/**aftaad-o-yak**/ "seventy-one"

/"**ashtaad**/ "eighty"

/**nawad**/ "ninety"

/**nawad-o-yak**/ "ninety-one"

/**sad**/ "hundred"

/**yaksad-o-yak**/ "one hundred and one"

/**azaar**/ "thousand"

/lak/ "one hundred thousand"

/**yag azaar-o-yak**/ "one thousand and one"

/**melyun**/ "million"

Note that, {-wo-} and {-o-} are variants of {wa}. The former is used after a vowel and the latter after a consonant.

II. Ordinal Numbers With the exception of the first one, an Arabic word, the rest of the ordinal numbers are made by adding {-om} after a consonant, or{-wom}after a vowel to a cardinal number.

/**awal**/ "first"

/**seywom**/ "third"

/**panjom**/ "fifth"

/**aftom**/ "seventh"

/**dowom**/ "second"

/**chaarom**/ "fourth"

/**shashom**/ "sixth"

/**ashtom**/ "eighth" and so on.

Superlative Ordinal Numbers

Like adjectives, ordinal numbers also have the superlative form when the suffix {in} is added. Thus /awal/ "second," and /awalin/ "a first," /dowom / "second, and /dowomin/ "second," and so on. Unlike ordinal numbers which can precede and follow nouns, superlative ordinal numbers only precede them. Hence, /awalin rayis-e jamur-e amrikaa/ means "The first president of the United States of America." But not */rayis-e jamur-e awalin-e amrikaa/.

APPENDIX C

Afghan Names

Most Afghans have one name at birth, but later on prefixes and suffixes can also be added. One's name at birth may consist of one or two words that cannot be broken into two or doubled. Thus, "Abdullah" (slave of God), is one word in Dari but in Arabic it is two: "abd" (slave) and "Allah" (God). "Mohammad Ehsan," on the other hand, is made up of two words. Even though it consists of two words, it cannot be broken into "Mohammad" and "Ehsan" as first and last names, as is customary in the West. It is somewhat strange to call a person with this name as "Ehsan" in Afghanistan. Therefore, it is better to think of "Mohammad-Ehsan" hyphenated so that they can be a unit. Similarly, when a name consists of only one word, it cannot be doubled in order to fit the name system in the West. Thus, calling someone as "Abdullah Abdullah" is just as strange as "Ehsan." By the same token, it is also inappropriate to break "Abdullah" into "Abd" and "Ullah."

Most names given to a new born baby have their origins in the Arabic language mentioned in the Koran. The majority of the Arabic names are related to God and his ninety-nine attributes: the Prophet Mohammad, his family and companions, and early leaders of Islam. When it comes to God's attributes, female names lack the prefix "Abd" or "Mohammad." Thus, "Mohammad Halim" is a male name, while "Halima" a female. Similarly, "Karim" is a boy's name but "Karima" is a girl's (The suffix {-a} is the feminine marker in Arabic). Names provided here are those of males unless indicated otherwise.

The Koran and other scriptures provide prophetic names such as **Maryam** "Mary,": **Eshaq** "Isaac," **Esa** "Jesus," **Musa** "Moses," [7] **Ebrahim** "Abraham,"

---

[7] There are various English transliterations of these names. Thus, Ebrahim or

154

Yaqub "Jacob," **Esmail** "Ishmail," **Adam** "Adam" as in Adam Khan, **Hawa** "Eve," **Yousuf** (Joseph), and so on.

A. Names at Birth (One Name)

1. **Mohammad +Prophetic Name**
   Mohammad Eshaq, Mohammad Ebrahim, Mohammad Yaqub, Mohammad Esmail, Mohammad Esa, Mohammad Musa, and so on.

2. **Noun+Allah.** "God"
   Nur "light" + Allah= Nurullah "The light of God"
   Najib "noble"+ Allah= Najibullah
   Sharif "noble"+Allah= Sharifullah "Noble of God"
   Qudrat "Power"+Allah+ Qudratullah "Power of God"
   Khalil "friend"+Allah= Khalilullah "Friend of God"
   Safee "pure, chosen"+Allah= Safiullah "The chosen of God"
   Mohammad "praiseworthy" +Allah = Mohammadullah "Praiseworthy of God"

3. **Noun+Mohammad ("The Prophet")**
   Khair "good/blessing" +Mohammad= Khair-Mohammad "Blessing of God"
   Dur "Pearl"+Mohammad= Dur-Mohammad "Pearl of Mohammad"
   Nazar "vision"+Mohammad= Nazar-Mohammad "Vision of Mohammad
   Gul "flower"+Mohammad= Gul-Mohammad "Flower of Mohammad"
   Nur "light"+ Mohammad=Nur-Mohammad "Light of Mohammad"
   Ghulam "Slave in Persian"+Mohammad= Ghulam-Mohammad "Slave of Mohammad"

4. **Mohammad+ Sahaba (Mohammad's Companions)**
   Mohammad +Abubakr (First Caliph) = Mohammad-Abubakr
   Mohammad+ Omar (Second Caliph) = Mohammad-Omar
   Mohammad +Osman (Third Caliph) = Mohammad-Osman
   Mohammad+Ali (Fourth Caliph) = Mohammad-Ali

5. **Abd/Mohammad+God's Attributes**
   Abd+Jabar "avenger"=Abdul-Jabar "Slave of the Avenger"
   Mohammad-Jabar Abd+Karim "generous" = Abdul-Karim, ("al" pronounced "ul" in Dari) is "Slave of the Generous"
   Mohammad-Karim Abd+Halim "forbearing"= Adul-Halim,

Ibrahim. However, in Dari script they are the same.

"Slave of the Forbearing"
Mohammad Karim Abd+Rahim "merciful"=Abdul-Rahim,
"Slave of the Merciful"
Mohammad-Rahim Abd+Qhahar "tyrant"=Abdul-Qhar,
"Slave of the Tyrant"

6. **From the Prophet Family**
Most Shiite Afghans choose names of their Imams (Ali Ibn Abutalib is their first and al-Mehdi the last). Among the Shiite men, **Ali, Hassan, Hussein** (Ali's sons), **Jafar,** and others are common names: Mohammad Ali, Mohammad Hussein, Mohammad Hassan, Hassan Ali etc. Shi'I women choose names of the Imams' wives and daughters as their names at birth: **Zahra, Fatima,** etc. It should be noted that, some Sunnis also have such names. What is certain is that a Shi'I man rarely, if ever, picks **Abubakr, Umar,** or **Osman** (names of the first three Caliphs) as their given names. The reason is that, they consider the first three Caliphs as illegitimate rulers of early Islam.

7. **From Legends and History**
Not all Afghan names are Arabic. Some names are also Persian with their origins in legends and history: Shirin (Female), Farhad, Yousuf, and Zulaikha (F), Rustam and Sorab, Layly (F) and Majnoon, Anahita (F), Changez (Ghingis Khan), and Sekandar (Alexander). **Thus,** Mohammad-Farhad, Mohammad-Rustam, Mohammad-Sorab, Majnoon-Shah, Mohammad-Yousuf, Mir-Hamza, and others.

8. **From Foreign Languages**
Diana, Nadiya (perhaps Russian), Endera (Hindi), and Mary (English) are some examples of female names.

9. **From nature**
The origins of some Afghan names can also be found in nature: Sher (lion), Nargis (narcissus), Gul (flower), Bulbul (nightingale), Tooty (parrot), Babrak/babur (tiger), Helay (duck in Pashto), Mahtab (moon in Persian), Qamar (moon in Arabic), Aftab (sun in Persian), Shams (sun in Arabic), Sitara (F) (star in Persian), Roshan (M/F) (light in Persian), Sabza (F) (grass in Persian), Almas (diamond), Parwana (F/M) (butterfly), Cheragh (light in Persian), Zia (light in Arabic). Thus, Sher Mohammad, Gul Mohammad, Bulbul Shah, Mahtabudin, Qamarudin, Aftabudin, Mohamad-Almas, Nargis (F), Helay (F), Gulbadan (F), and Sitara (F).

10. **From the Blessing of God**

When a couple cannot have a child, or it dies in infancy, and finally gets one or it wants a son after a couple of girls, they name their new born differently. Thus: Bubani (F) (May you live, Persian), Khuday Berdi (May God keep him alive, Persian-Turkish), Ehsanullah (favor of God), Mohammad Ehsan (favor of the Prophet), Enayatullah (divine favor), Shokrullah (grace of God), and so on.

11. **From Qualities of Good Men**

Delawar Khan (brave +chief or leader), Touryalay (brave in Pashto), Zalamy (Young in Pashto), Shujaudin (brave +religion)

B. Prefixes and Suffixes

As it has been pointed out, Afghan names at birth can later on have prefixes and suffixes. The former involves, titles of religions or professions, while the latter have to do with ethnicity, region, ideology, and so on.

1. **Prefixes**

a) **Sayed +Name** A male descendant of the Prophet Mohammad is called "sayed" which is added before a male's name. Thus, Sayed Mohammad-Akram, Sayed-Abdullah, and so on.

b) **Haji+Name**

A person having performed the Hajj becomes a Haji. Thus, Haji Mohammad-Akram, **Haji** Abdullah, and so on. A female who has returned from Mecca is called Bebi Haji, not * "Haji Karima."

c) **Occupation+Name**

One can also be called by his profession or trade. For example, a reciter of the Koran is a "Qari" as in **Qari Abdullah**. Similarly, a cleric who leads prayers, is a Mullah-**Mullah Omar,** and one leading prayers at a big mosque is a Mawlawi**Mawlawi Mohammad Akbar.** A teacher "malem" is called **Malem MohammadAta,** or just Malem Ata, a university professor is called Ustad as in **Ustad Rabbani, Qazi Hussein** (Judge Hussein), **Khalifa Kabir** (drivers, carpenters and others highly skilled are referred to "Khalifa," Mirza (scriber) Miralam (Miralam the scriber).

2. Suffixes

Last names are a relatively recent phenomenon in Afghanistan. Mustafa Kamal, known as Ataturk "Father of Turkey," was probably the first ruler who made last names obligatory in his country. In the Islamic countries, Afghanistan and Iran tried to adopt his modernization efforts. Adopting last names may have been such an imitation in Afghanistan. The roots of Afghan last names are ethnicity, place of birth, ideology, and others.

a) **Ethnicity**
   Ethnicity refers to race and language. Some Afghans want to identify with their ethnic groups, including tribe and clan: Khalid **Pashtun** (ethnicity), Ahmad-Shah **Durrani** (tribe), Hamid **Karzai** (clan), Abdullah **Baloch** (ethnicity), and Seddiq **Popal** (clan). Names related to a tribe or clan are more common among the Pashtuns who take Nasab (genealogy) seriously.

b) **Place of Birth**
   Some Afghans want to identify with their place of birth: Akhtar-Mohammad **Paktiyawall** (from Paktia), Dastagir **Panjshiri** (from Pajnjshir), Daud **Nuristani** (from Nuristan), Abdul-Ali **Mazari** (from Mazar-e Sahrif), Mahir **Herawi** (from Herat), Durai **Logari** (from Logar), Latif **Nangarhari** (from Nangarhar), Sayyed Jamaludin **Afghani** (from Afghanistan), and so on.

c) **Ideology/philosophy**
   Some last names express one's ideology. The last name "Kargar" (laborer) as in Karim Kargar, for example, has the connotation of being a leftist. A Pashto example of this is Abdullah Ziyarmal (Lit. friend of the working class).

d). **Random and Subjective**
   Other last names are subjective and have no logical explanation. My last name, for example, is "Entezar" (wait). I have no idea why I picked this particular word as my last name. What is clear, however, is that I simply wanted to be distinguished from tens of thousands of other "Mohammad Ehsans" in Afghanistan. This is because, at the time, I began writing articles for publication in Kabul. And when I came to the United States, I had to change my first name "Mohammad" to "Ehsan" because Americans kept calling me "Mohammad." My sons' names also begin with "Mohammad": Mohammad Fareed Entezar,

Mohammad Najeeb Entezar, and Mohammad Waheed Entezar. Some other Afghans, when in America change their first names to "Mike," "David," and others for reasons other than avoiding confusion. Thus "**David** Kakar," "**Joe** Kohistani," and so on.

C. Laqab or Nick Name

The word "laqab" is an Arabic word meaning "title," but it can be used in the sense of "honorary title," bestowed upon a male or female, by the family members or society. In an Afghan family, it is impolite for younger children to call their older siblings by their given names. Instead, they make use of *laqab* or nick names when addressing them. Such nicknames mostly contain words like /aaghaa/ "master," /sheyr/ "lion," /sherin/ "sweet," /jaan/ "dear,"/del/ "heart," /shaa/ "king," and /gol/ "flower." Common laqabs for males in an Afghan family include **Gulagha** (Lit. flower master), **Shirinagha** (sweet master), **Qandagha** (sweet master), **Shiragha** (lion master), **Delagha** (heart master), and so on. The female members have laqabs such as **Deljan** (dearheart), **Shiringul** (sweetflower), **Qandigul** (sugarflower), and so on. Such laqabs are usually known to the members of the immediate and extended families, but not to others. Finally, it is important to note that, laqabs when used in a family, are more common among the uneducated Afghans. Finally, it is worth noting that laqabs are also awarded to individuals for their great service to society. For example, "Father of the Nation" was the laqab given to the late King Zahir Shah as a symbol of national unity.

Index